W9-CIE-018

The net proceeds from the sale of this book
will be contributed by the publisher
to organizations specifically responding to the needs
of retired religious.

"If one wishes to understand religious life today—and its fluid situation—one needs to understand other critical changes in religious life in the course of history. Vatican II calls for a new kind of religious woman. No longer tied down to monastic practices required by the church in earlier times, sisters are now required to organize their lifestyle around the ministry they exercise. The author tells what renewal of religious life for women has meant."

Ernest Falardeau, S.S.
Emmanuel

"*From Nuns to Sisters* by Sister Marie Augusta, SND de Namur, deserves special attention. The author is well known as a sociologist of religion whose surveys of women in religious life over a more than twenty-year period constitute the largest data base ever assembled on the subject. Thus the trends studied in the present volume are not theoretical but derive from the author's sociological analysis of the 'renewal years' as reproted by the subjects themselves. The title is Sister Marie Augusta's shorthand designating the evolution of religious life from a semi-monastic orientation to a style the core of which is 'preferential option for the poor.' "

Anita Caspary, I.H.M.

"A sensitive, perceptive, and challenging analysis of the growth of United States women religious from nuns to sisters, Marie Augusta Neal's *From Nuns to Sisters* both carefully unfolds her subject matter...and skillfully probes her theme. Neal has the rare ability to synthesize succinctly broad sweeps of history without treating historical currents in a superficial manner.

"Marie Augusta Neal, mentor, model, and colleague for History of Women Religious members, has given us another outstanding study, one aptly suited for courses in the history of women religious, theology of religious life and the vows, or for personally challenging reading."

Regina Siegfried, A.S.C.
Aquinas Institute, St. Louis

"The book is a celebration of the conciliar spirit of women religious. It is an investigation into the religious vows, their renewal, and a re-examination of congregational life....Neal's discussion of women's 'expanding vocation' is well-founded, convincing, and very encouraging."

Paul Matthew St. Pierre
The B.C. Catholic

"This examination of the changing vowed life is based on the largest data base ever assembled on women religious. The changes it examines seem to point back to the early constitutions of the orders, recognizing the church's continuing option for the poor. The transitions studied here challenge the structure of governance we have known in the church and in religious communities."

National Catholic Reporter

"Although this book records the pattern of women's religious life over the centuries, the centrality of the vows in that way of life, and the restrictions placed upon it, *From Nuns to Sisters* is far from being simply a history. The subtitle, *An Expanding Vocation*, indicates its scope. Neal does not evade the problems of the prophetic ministry of transforming the world in justice. She believes altruism is the ultimate purpose of the vowed life of sisters: love of neighbor before self-interest. The call of the poor cannot be ignored. Critical social analysis followed by action are required of sisters today."

Teresa White, F.C.J.
Religious Life Review

"...a clear presentation of the development of religious life and a service to those who study religious life and its role in the church. Perhaps the best part is Neal's clear, unemotional, insightful look at the tensions among religious orders today, which are caught between responding to changing times, the decrees of Vatican II, and a sense that church authorities are trying to reverse the momentum that has marked post-World War II society."

Sister Mary Ann Walsh
Catholic News Service

MARIE AUGUSTA NEAL, SND de NAMUR

from
NUNS
to
SISTERS
AN EXPANDING
VOCATION

XXIII
TWENTY-THIRD PUBLICATIONS
Mystic, Connecticut

Third printing 1990

Twenty-Third Publications
185 Willow Street
P.O. Box 180
Mystic, CT 06355
(203) 536-2611

ISBN 0-89622-400-7
Library of Congress Catalog Card Number 89-51579

Acknowledgments

This study was begun during a sabbatical year in 1983 but has undergone many modifications since that time. The first chapter, "From Nuns to Sisters," was presented as a lecture in the Women's Studies in Religion program at Harvard Divinity School in the spring of 1983. The second chapter, "Prophetic Ministry and Risk," was first presented as a paper in a series entitled "Women, Religion, and Social Change," at the Center for the Study of World Religions, Harvard University, March 7, 1983. It was later revised and published in *Studies in Formative Spirituality*, Vol. 5, No. 3, November 1984, and in its current form is a revision of that version. The other three chapters appear here for the first time.

The time to do the research for this study was granted to me by Emmanuel College, Boston, through an appointment as professor of sociology for research and teaching. I want to express my deep gratitude to Sister Janet Eisner, S.N.D, president of Emmanuel College, for this appointment which made possible the continuation of the research on sisters.

I would like to dedicate this book to women who have been willing to serve as administrators in religious congregations during this period of transition, to those who are not only witnesses to the shift from individual authority to the struggle of the poor to get authority, but also participants in the development of a new appreciation for administering, coordinating, facilitating, and supporting. So to Sisters Esther MacCarthy, Mary T. Kelleher, and Nancy Rowen, this study is lovingly dedicated. Let these names stand also for those of all the women religious who have been leaders in the recent past and who will be called to lead in settings where the rules are not clear, the responsibilities great, submissive members few but colleagues many. My gratitude to my faithful editor, Sister Grace Pizzimenti, is beyond measure. Thanks too to Jennifer Oberg, a colleague from the 1960s, for insightful comments, and to Joanne Beserdetsky and Melissa Hall for accepting enthusiastically the adventure of learning word processing in order to do the typing for this book, along with their many other research tasks.

From Nuns to Sisters is dedicated also to three Sisters of Notre Dame who, in their lives of deep commitment, creative service, and day-to-day participation in a life of mission and community, evidence where the paths are being drawn: Mary Johnson, Patricia O'Brien, and Joan Ellen Hurley. Let them represent all the unnamed newer members of religious congregations, those women of the present and those of the future who hear a call to mission and seek a community of sisters through which to realize it. That call to mission will be realized in different ways in apostolic congregations whose histories and charisms each have their own unique forms and which are constantly challenged to respond in creative ways to the signs of the times and the call of the church.

Contents

Acknowledgments   *vii*

Introduction   1
The Option for the Poor: From Alleviation to Elimination • Renewal of Formation • Research Evidence • Themes by Chapter • Current Dilemmas

1 From Nuns to Sisters:Three Significant Changes   9
The Transition• Three Different Forms of the Religious Calling • The Contemplative and Semi-Contemplative Life • Option for the Poor • Period I: Early Christian Era to 1600 • Vowed Virginity, A New Way of Life for Women • Deaconesses and Widows • Emergence of Convent Life for Women • The Decline and Fall • The Cloister • Period II: 1600 to 1950 • The Cloister or Good Works • Poverty or Property • Daughters of Charity • Doers of Good Works • Period III: 1950 to the Present • The Formation of Nuns and Sisters • The Emergence of Modern Sisters • Critical Social Analysis • Obedience to the Mission of the Church

2 Prophetic Ministry and Risk   39
One Hundred Years of Vatican Teaching • The Office of Justice and Peace • Social Sin • From Radical Critique to Church Mandate • Formation for a Justice Mission • The Call to Mission

3 Constitutions and Mission   52
Guidelines for Renewal • The Sisters' Survey • Conflict Within • Statements of Mission in the Light of the Council • Some Expressions of the New Perspective on Mission • The New Challenge • Participation in Decision Making

4 Vows in the Context of Mission   67

   The Purpose of the Vowed Life • The Modern Context of the
   Vowed Life • The Place of Altruism in Modern Society • Current Challenges to Altruistic Service • Institutionalization of
   the Vowed Life • New Focus of the Vow of Obedience • Canonical Definition of the Vows in General • The Vow of Chastity • Convent Living • The Vow of Poverty • The Vow of Obedience • Current Challenges to the Vow of Obedience • Strains
   on Administrators in Religious Communities • Another Dilemma

5 Governance and the Realization of Mission   89

   Governance for Mission • Limitations in the Canons • A New
   Dynamic • Archaic Language • Uses of Authority • Structures
   of Government • Preference for and Perceptions of Forms of
   Government • Preferred Forms of Decision Making • Perceived Forms of Decision Making • The Tale of One Congregation • Another Tale • The Sanctity of Personal Authority •
   Government as a Form of Witness for Mission • Faith and Organization

Epilogue   114

   Shedding the Carapace • Youth and Mission • The Call to
   Congregational Religious Life

Notes   120
Bibliography   132

INTRODUCTION

The Option for the Poor:
From Alleviation to Elimination

What does it mean to have a special option for the poor? How do we announce the Good News to the poor? How is God announced to us through the poor? What happens to the non-poor with all this new concern for the poor?

These questions have become central issues in the General Chapters of Catholic sisters in the more than twenty years since the Second Vatican Council. The striking changes that have been made over these years in the institutional patterns of the past are a function of the emphasis the church has given to the struggles of the poor, particularly as they organize themselves to claim their rights as human beings. How and why these changes have occurred and what their relationships are to this urgent mission of today's church, is the subject matter of this book. Within clearly identifiable historical, sociocultural, and theological processes, some nuns have become sisters, leaving seclusion and security to embark upon an uncharted path of change and risk in response to the church's call. As a partial consequence of the Second Vatican Council (1962-1965), the Catholic church has refocused its mission to the poor. Prior to the Second Vatican Council, works of charity on the part of those with resources were the central means of doing the church's mission. Since the council, however, acts of social justice that seek to eliminate the causes of poverty have become central goals (see Synod, 1971). This new emphasis has finally brought to the fore the reality of the jubilee and the sabbatical in their original biblical meaning:

namely that, since the land belongs to the people, they cannot be dispossessed of it in perpetuity (Leviticus 25:23).

During the mid-twentieth century, developments in science and technology, and in social analysis and literacy among the peoples of the world, revealed the fact that there is no so-called natural hierarchy wherein some are destined to rule and to own the wealth, and others to work the land and to be cared for out of the largesse of natural elites. The realization that human rights belong to all human beings gradually replaced the erroneous assumptions about the natural evolution of psychic, moral and mental distinctions within the human race. In addition, many began to recognize that these flawed assumptions of the natural human superiority and inferiority undergird socioeconomic structures which have served to perpetuate the advantage of some groups and the misery of others.

The council recognized that the gospel of Christianity, institutionalized through the centuries into services of health, education and welfare works, had become deeply entangled, sometimes unwittingly, with the assumptions of these natural hierarchies of competency and heritage. As a consequence, a general restructuring was needed to free the church and its mission from unjust customs and exploitation. A growing awareness of this need had begun to develop well before the council and had contributed to the impetus to call it. To accomplish this task of renewal, Pope John XXIII, a man of "peasant stock," announced the council in 1962 and specified its function as that of an *aggiornamento*, an updating of the church in keeping with the signs of the times, namely, the alarming number of poor and oppressed peoples of the world. Third World missionaries, especially from Brazil and other Latin American countries, but also those from Africa and Asia, provided much of the evidence of this struggle. Pope John XXIII had already written about it in *Mater et Magistra* in 1961, noting that the church in Latin America was far too closely linked with oppressive political economies. He further elaborated this theme in *Pacem in Terris* (1963) wherein he claimed that peace, poverty and human rights are the central concerns of committed Christians everywhere.

As previously noted, after the church developed the implications of its mission, its programs became directed more to the *elimination* of the causes of poverty than, as had been true formerly, to the *alleviation* of its results. As the church moved from close support of established systems to a basic challenge of those same systems, no group was more deeply affected by this new emphasis than Catholic sisters throughout the world but most especially in the United States.

Renewal of Formation

At mid-century, guided by mandates issued by Pope Pius XII, the religious congregations of women and of men had moved out of their enclosures to assess their professional competencies for the apostolic services they were providing in health, education, and welfare. They met together internationally in convocations as major superiors, as teachers and as formation directors in Rome in the early fifties. These gatherings, the first of their kind in history, brought together religious order and congregation members to compare and critique both their works and the formation of their members for their work. The most important result of this evaluation was the planned upgrading of formal education for new members. For women religious in massive numbers, this meant the first systematic formalization of their training into academic degree programs. The providing of degrees and of competent training gave members a new independence. For this very pragmatic reason, while some sisters became freer to make choices to leave their congregations, at the same time many more women chose to become sisters, admittedly attracted by the formation program itself.

But increase in competency was not the only change affecting members of religious congregations of women in the fifties. New theologies which emphasized social responsibility, motivational awareness, respect for the intellectual life and for human rights were being published and circulated throughout Europe and North America. (See de Lubac 1951, Chenu 1957, Congar 1957; also Neal 1965.) These theologies were questioned by the

Congregation of the Doctrine of the Faith and were allowed only limited circulation. However, through channels like *Cross Currents* and other documentary services, they were translated into English and found their way directly into the new religious formation programs of Catholic sisters in the United States during the 1950s. An exciting ferment developed among the younger women in training for religious life when these materials were used. It focused on the new social justice emphasis in the church. When these same theologians then became the periti at the Second Vatican Council, the formation programs in many Catholic sisters' congregations were at the forefront in understanding the significance of the council in the new life of the church.

How this ferment became a radical transition point in the experience of religious congregations of Catholic women, especially in the United States, is the theme of this book. The evidence for this exploration is provided by substantial survey and data analysis that the author gathered, first on Catholic priests between 1958 and 1962, and then on Catholic sisters from 1965 onward. Although it is not possible in the scope of this book to present detailed analyses of these surveys, it is useful to cite and to identify them here as the instruments used to generate the data for and to establish the validity of the conclusions reached in this study.

Research Evidence

The data on priests, limited to respondents within the Archdiocese of Boston, have been published in *Values and Interests in Social Change* (1965). The data compiled on sisters, the most comprehensive data of their kind, underlies a research study consisting of several parts. The first part is a congregational survey, distributed through the Conference of Major Superiors of Women Religious (CMSW) in 1966. This was responded to by one administrator from each of 437 different units of 301 different religious congregations. This was followed in 1982 by a retest of this same population to which 342 congregations responded. These data were analyzed and published in 1984 in

Catholic Sisters in Transition from the 1960s to the 1980s.

The second part of that study, known as *The Sisters' Survey*, was constructed in l966 to determine the readiness of sisters to implement the decisions of the Second Vatican Council. In 1967, it was sent out to all the religious women represented in the CMSW—157,000 individuals—and 139,691 responded to it. These data, analyzed in several ways, were then circulated to each congregation.

The materials sent included a comparative analysis of their own responses to the 649 questions and the scales these included, with a national profile of all the respondents' scores. The data were cross-tabulated with several census variables, as well as with attitude and opinion scales, the best known of which is a pre- and post-Vatican belief scale (see Neal 1971, 1972). These data were re-tested in l980 on a selected group of twenty congregations, chosen for their range of reponses to this belief scale and randomly sampled within each congregation. Some analyses of those data have been published in several journal articles and book chapters referred to in this text. In 1989, a third sisters' survey was circulated to a random sample of 3000 drawn from the membership lists of 91,900 of all sisters' congregations in the United States. The results will be published within the next two years and will include the data from all three surveys examining the influence of religious belief on social behavior.

The third part of the study, begun in 1974, includes a systematic analysis of constitutions being revised in 280 different religious congregations. In 1983, the later interim constitutions of twenty congregations studied in detail were analyzed. The coding categories for the analysis of these constitutions were derived from the documents of the Second Vatican Council and subsequent social analysis documents of the church. These findings are not yet published. An update of this analysis, using the final constitution revisions, will be part of the final study. The basic purpose of the entire study is to determine the degree of commitment of women religious to the mission of the church, as highlighted by Vatican II, regarding social justice and an option for the poor.

The findings from these three parts of the study of religious congregations of women provide the findings from which the present work is developed. These findings will be referred to where relevant, but will not be recorded in these essays. An overview of the chapter content of this book may serve to set its perspective, context and framework, with the first chapter receiving fuller attention here because of the lengthy historical background it presents.

Themes by Chapter

Chapter 1 argues that there have been three major transitions in the emergence of apostolic religious congregations in the Catholic church and that women have played a major role in each of them. The vows of religious life have been focal in each transition and are linked to the contemporaneous changes in major institutions of European society.

The vow of chastity, as part of the first transition, when initially suggested in the early church, was considered an unacceptable choice for women, whose identity was perceived as entirely linked to the extended family. However, this vow, in time, gave women an identity separate from that which identified them with the family. The legitimization of this change took some four hundred years (McNamara 1983). The second major transition was economic and related to the vow of poverty and the institution of property inheritance (Power 1975). This phase ended only with the lifting of the cloister as a requisite for religious life for women in the church. This took 600 years. The third major transition, closely related to the first two, is political and relates to the vow of obedience and the structure of governance. This transition, only now in process, is challenging the very structure of the church in the modern world, most particularly in terms of the mission to which the church has explicitly committed itself through the last hundred years of Vatican teaching, namely, the special option for the poor (Dorr 1983). As with every major transition in the life of the church, this one is directly related to the role of women in society at large and to the role of all oppressed peoples in the world. The recognition of the emergent rights of the dispossessed to share in the rich resources of the world (not through the magnanimity of those who claim control over them, but by reason of their own human rights) mandates the necessity of all peoples to participate in the decisions that affect their lives. But, to make such a transition in governance, one must structure governance to meet this need. This is the challenge which religious women, in their understanding of mission and commitment to it, make to their church today.

Chapter 2 examines how the doing of this mission of justice for the poor is accomplished, along with the risks thereby incurred. Chapter 3 considers how the new constitutions of religious congregations of women express this mission and propose structures for implementing it. Chapter 4 looks at the way the vows have been adapted to the mission; Chapter 5, the effect the mission has on structures of governance in religious congregations and the implications and dangers involved in this change.

Where sisters are going, there is no path. But one is even now being made, its direction for mission set by increasingly clear options and choices. And so the journey is perilous and the risks real.

Current Dilemmas

There are practical problems to be dealt with, it is true. Religious congregations are caught up at the present moment in the dilemmas posed by an aging membership, by declining numbers of new members in the United States and Europe, and by the pragmatics of solving problems of finances and formation. Unfortunately, these problems obscure the dynamics of and deflect public attention from the more profound and compelling drama of a religious calling that seeks and suggests radical changes in the very structure of modern society. In the Third World, vocations to religious life are generally increasing, especially in Africa and Asia. Those who have wondered where all the sisters have gone will find them in the most unlikely places, still committed to a common mission but quite divided as to how to realize it effectively.

An important aspect of sisters' lives is the communal context in which they live and from which they draw psychic energy and support. However, community life becomes vulnerable to ambition and idiosyncratic aspiration, once the range of options is extended and participation in decision making opened to all members. Making authentic community, therefore, remains a central value among those committed to the vowed life. The test of whether or not this is being done will be the focus of further research; the focus in this book is on the relationship between commitment to a mission and the putting in place of structures for its implementation.

—1—

From Nuns to Sisters: Three Significant Changes

At a renewal meeting which I attended in the early 1970s, Sister Jon Julie Sullivan, formerly a fourth grade teacher, a college chaplain, and later a carer for children in a single-parent home, opened a reflection session saying: "I am an ex-nun." Her fellow sisters looked up startled, some expecting a formal announcement that she was leaving the congregation; others, knowing her penchant for surprising introductions, waited expectantly for some significant observation. It came. "When I joined the Sisters of Notre Dame, I was attracted by the long, flowing garments, the rosary beads that were more than ornaments, that stood for something beyond the ordinary. I liked getting up at dawn, meditating for a whole hour before Mass. I liked the silence, the discipline of the regular life, all the wonderful customs that set us apart, alone with God. I liked the contemplative life. Most of it is gone now. I am still here among my sisters but I am not yet a sister. I am an ex-nun." She stopped and sat down. We pondered what she had said. She got up again. "Don't get me wrong, I like being a sister but I am not there yet."

What was she saying? Her life was a witness to her commitment to mission. Yet it seems that what she was saying was that the transition, from a nun to a sister, was hard for her. What this transition encompasses is the subject matter of this chapter.

The Transition

There are almost a million Catholic single women in the world who are members of religious orders or congregations. Some of them are called nuns, and others sisters. Nuns used to live in convents or monasteries and wore uniform garb called religious habits. Their life was carefully regulated by a daily *horarium*, punctuated by periods of meditation and by the recitation of the prayer of the church, the Liturgy of the Hours. Although, until the early 1960s, some of these women might be seen walking along the streets quietly in pairs, others lived their entire lives cloistered in a walled monastery. Few people knew the distinction between a nun and a sister, though they did know that sisters usually taught school, worked as nurses in hospitals, cared for elderly people in their homes and in institutions established for this purpose, and performed other works of mercy and charity. Some might even have known that the nuns sang the Liturgy of the Hours and meditated and that a few had, on occasion, experienced ecstasy and other mystical forms of direct encounter with God. Although both nuns and sisters were perceived to be dedicated to God through the vows of poverty, chastity and obedience, to some observers nuns may have seemed, in their total withdrawal from the world, to have a vocation more spiritual than that of the sisters, who were more in the active world, even if still somewhat withdrawn from it.

In recent years, some sisters have made news internationally by being killed in Third World countries, where the local people are struggling to free themselves from oppressive governments resisting land reform. The best known of these cases involved the deaths of four Americans in El Salvador in December 1980: three religious sisters, Maura Clark, Dorothy Kazel, and Ita Ford, and one lay volunteer, Jeanne Donovan (see Chapter 2). When this event occurred, the news media attempted to explain to the public who nuns and sisters and lay volunteers were, because the event raised the question in the public mind. Media personnel sought explanations that the scholarly literature could not yet provide, because the roles of nuns and sisters were, at the time, in the process of major transformation. In fact, the three types of commitment—that of the contemplative nun, the apostolic sister and the lay volunteer—are historical products that are linked in interesting ways to the life of the church. This link is related to the history of Christianity, as it developed in Europe and North Africa, and then spread to the rest of the world. It is particularly related to the differential roles of women in society, and to the relation of the church to the state and the economy.

Three Different Forms of the Religious Calling

In the scope of one chapter, I can present only a segment of this linkage, as discernible in the roles of nuns and sisters. Here I will develop the thesis that, throughout history, the tension between good works and prayer—two components of the religious calling—has had three strikingly different forms in the creation of institutions for single women responding to a religious calling in the Catholic church. Each of these forms has emerged in a particular socio-economic milieu. Transitions in the larger structures of these socio-economic contexts generated the environment for change in the forms of life for nuns and sisters in three historical periods: 1) the early Christian era to 1600; 2) 1600 to 1950; 3) 1950 to the present.

The Contemplative and Semi-Contemplative Life

Before exploring the historical record, let us look briefly here at the two concepts of religious life subsumed in the vocations of "nun" and of "sister." The first form, that of the contemplative vocation, gives a clear and unambiguous primacy to prayer in a monastery or convent setting of almost total exclusion of non-members. This calling dominated the vocation of single women in the early medieval church of Europe and North Africa. The second form combined the doing of good works and the performance of traditional prayer forms. This semi-contemplative life characterized convent living from the seventeenth century through 1950. In this form, the model for prayer remained that of the monastic community: the centuries-old routine of daily singing or reciting the Divine Office, an hour and a half of daily meditation, attendance at Mass and other required communal and private prayers, and periodic gatherings for meals, reading, instruction, and physical labor. This schedule, adopted by sisters in the semi-contemplative life, was fitted into the varied demands of teaching, nursing and other social services. In this historical period, these services, provided in highly institutionalized ways, were offered in buildings either attached or immediately adjacent to the convents and belonging to the religious congregation, or to the parish or diocese in which they were located. In the course of time, this institutionalization both routinized the services and established distances, required by the cloister, between the serving sisters and the serviced poor, and others as well. The combination of the cloister, the religious habit, and the regular life of prayer and community surrounded religious life with an aura of order and calm. It also in time, however, affected the quality of the human services given, subordinating them as secondary in importance to the sound of the bell calling the sisters to prayer. Obedience to the sound of the bell was considered obedience to the will of God. It remained for the Sister Formation Movement and the Second Vatican Council, in the third historical period, 1950 to the present, to complete the changes essential to the new ministries undertaken by sisters.

Option for the Poor

The renewal of the church, introduced by the Second Vatican Council, convened by Pope John XXIII in 1963, formalized a new but already developing theological orientation. It marked a radical transition in the services undertaken by Catholic sisters and a clearer distinction between the vocation of nuns and that of sisters in the church. This change resulted from a formal decision the Catholic church made at the Second Vatican Council to stand in solidarity with the poor of the world. The agenda of the council was converted into a worldwide call to effective action for the transformation of unjust social institutions and structures. The church, thereafter, made its option increasingly explicit, striving to implement actions of justice and peace in various parts of the world.[1] One formulation of the new theological stance adopted stated:

> Inherent in our developing understanding of mission is the belief that God who is revealed in many ways calls to us with special insistence through the voices of the poor as they seek to organize themselves to claim their rights as human beings.[2]

This dominant focus on the struggles of the poor to organize themselves to claim their rights as human beings can be seen in the 1980s in the cooperation among missionaries of many denominations. Many such groups spoke out in support of Central American, Southern African and Southeast Asian peoples' efforts to withstand the control exerted by activities of transnational corporations and first and second world imperialism (Arruda 1980).[3] The moral challenge such a confrontation presents to the church in the late twentieth century and the adaptations being made to meet this challenge, parallel previous threats to the moral order that faced the early church. At first, it confronted and then adapted to the Roman Empire. Later, the early modern church similarly opposed and then accepted the new nation states and the industrial revolution in seventeenth century Europe. In reflecting on the dynamics of new forms of religious life and their subsequent institutionalization into the vocation of the single woman in the vowed life, it is useful to look at each of these earlier periods in sequence, as a way to understand more clearly the present situation of nuns and sisters in the United States.

Period I: Early Christian Era to 1600

Writing of women in classical antiquity, Sarah Pomeroy titles her book, *Goddesses, Whores, Wives and Slaves,* for these were the main roles she found assigned to women of ancient Rome and

Greece. In ancient Israel, the good woman affirmed in the Bible was wife and mother. Her virtue was extolled if she could manage a household, weave cloth for her family, servants and slaves, and tend the farm when her husband was away (Vos 1968). Later, her religious role was expanded but still limited to lighting the candles for the Friday night home service, and to being responsible for the observance of the fasts and dietary rules in the home. At no time could she function as part of the worship service in the temple or in the synagogue (Hauptman 1974). This restriction protected her primary function of motherhood, just as it did in Rome and Greece where being wife and mother were also the roles esteemed for women. In none of these cultures was there an independent status role for single women in any social structure and, in the state religion especially, she had no accepted religious role, with the possible exception of that of prophet (Vos, p. 208).

Elisabeth Schüssler Fiorenza, who has studied the role of women in religion in early Christian times, concludes that Jesus, in bearing witness to a more egalitarian church, created the possibility for public roles for women. St. Paul, writing to the Galatians, suggested that, in this new church, old divisions would disappear and there would be neither Jew nor Greek, slave nor free, male nor female, but all would be one in Christ Jesus (Galatians 3:28). Fiorenza observes that there are recorded instances in which women presided at house-church meetings where Eucharist was celebrated and was followed by a community meal. The later Christian communities, she discovers, however, gradually became patriarchal, as they modeled themselves on the surrounding Hellenic and Judaic cultures of the day rather than on the New Testament scriptural model (Fiorenza 1970, 1983).

Vowed Virginity, a New Way of Life for Women

There is substantial, even if derived, evidence that in the first three centuries of the church, women who felt called to follow Jesus outside the traditional roles of wife and mother banded together in vowed virginity to pray and do good works. This choice not to marry, though at first disturbing to the Fathers of the church, eventually became affirmed as a valued mode of holiness. This transition can be seen in Clement of Alexandria's early condemnation of the choice to remain single, Origen's later acceptance of it, and Tertullian's conversion to eulogizing it (McNamara 1983, 81-98).[4] Later Christian writers took this affirming position until the Protestant Reformation again condemned vowed virginity, even as Catholics enshrined it as a true road to sanctity for women. Jo Ann McNamara argues persuasively that women invented the celibate state as a Christian way of life two centuries *before* the church defined it as a superior means to achieve Christian perfection. Her careful historical study of the origin of the choice of virginity as a path to holiness in the church provides considerable substantiation of the thesis I am developing here: that the institutional form the vowed life takes in each historical era rises out of the major social structural strains of that era. This, accordingly, engenders resistance to the new form of the vowed life within the church, linked as it is to society at large, and caught within these strains.

In this first period, the structural strain, with regard to women and the vowed life, emerged in response to the absence of any legitimate role for women outside of the married state, as institutionalized in the Greek, Roman, and Jewish models operative at the time. Those models failed to take into account, as a possibility for women, the Christian invitation to follow Jesus according to the counsels of the beatitudes, which proposed, as one calling, *leaving all to follow him* (Mark 10:21). In her work, McNamara also demonstrates, as do many other writers using early Christian documents, that the restrictions placed on women who wished to lead such a life of Christian perfection soon became circumscribed by standard definitions of women as temptations in the path of religious men (Davies 1980, p. 89; Power 1975, p. 11; Boyd 1943, p. 73).

McNamara concludes, from a careful review of extant documents from the first three centuries of Christianity, that the idea of a calling to virginity is a totally Christian concept, fashioned by Roman women seeking to realize a Christian life distinct from that open to them through marriage. There were no unmarried Roman women, she notes. The life of celibacy became, shortly afterwards, a preferred path to holiness for Christian men also. However, its devising and the experimentation with it was a women's choice that the church sanctioned only after an initial rejection, a reluctant acceptance, and then a whole-hearted idealization (McNamara 1983).

Deaconessess and Widows

The choice of priesthood and the choice of the vowed life were two distinct vocations chosen by women. It would seem that the historical role of deaconess, a person who assisted the bishop in the sacramental function, developed from the kind of women's participation in the early church explored in Fiorenza's work. The role of nun, a vocation for single women, derived from subsequent efforts of women to pray and to serve in a communal context. The history of the first phase of women's active involvement in the church leads to an investigation of women in ordination (an aspiration not limited to single women); the history of the second phase, to the various forms of religious institutes of single women in the vowed life. Both roles for women, however, are embedded in a history of trends moving away from an early egalitarian church structure. The study of deaconesses reveals the decline to final extinction of that role in the Catholic tradition and then its later resurrection in Protestantism in the nineteenth century (Prelinger 1982, 1986). The study of nuns in the early years of their existence traces the development of community and cloister from the third through the fifth centuries (Ruether 1974). In the fifth century, the institution of convent life emerged for nuns. Prior to this time, the only two clearly defined religious roles for women in the church were those of widows and deaconesses. The order of widows functioned to pray and care for the sick; they also fasted on special occasions. Women over sixty who had been married only once and had lived a good life could join the order of widows, recognized as part of the formal structure of the church but distinguished from ordination (Danielou 1960). After this order declined, toward the end of the third century, there was an expansion of the role of deaconesses, active since the time of the apostles and later in-stitutionalized in the East through the laying on of hands. They performed functions characteristic of minor orders (Prelinger 1986). This order related to assisting the bishop, but only in his ministry to women. The work of the deaconess was mostly mis-sionary, that is, preaching the Gospel to heathen women but not making interpretations, a function jealously guarded for men (Fiorenza 1970, p. 43). Deaconesses were replaced by the clergy if they overstepped the boundaries of their roles by attempting to pronounce on theological questions (Danielou, p. 20). As not-ed, the role of deaconess declined in the fifth century but it did not disappear in the early church until the eleventh century. The role of the nun, however, assumed new importance as the ideal of virginity gradually became affirmed by the church. The choice of the celibate life attracted both men and women; yet it did not necessarily lead to ordination, according to developing church custom, but could do so in the case of men.

That there was some struggle on the part of churchmen for the right to exert religious power over women is evident. It is seen in the restrictions finally placed on the role of abbess, the ti-tle given to the woman in charge of a convent or monastery of nuns. As the power of the abbess extended, it was reduced and contained by council decree just as had happened earlier to each of the preceding roles of widow and deaconess (Danielou 1960). This was done by rules restricting travel outside the monastery, even by the abbess.

Emergence of Convent Life for Women

Examination of the writings concerning the convent life of nuns from the fifth century reveals that the religious elements valued in the new order of nuns included a somewhat narrow range of ascetic practices: extended time for prayer; refinement of liturgi-cal song for the singing of the Office in praise of God; fasting, meditation and spiritual reading. To assure that these spiritual exercises were observed, strict enclosure was mandated. Al-though some time was spent in daily manual labor, the pre-ferred works were those considered to be less distracting to the life of the spirit: reading, writing, spiritual reflection, meditation and copying manuscripts. The order of the day called for a strict lifestyle: early rising to intone the prayers of the Liturgy of the Hours, the discipline of sleeping in a common dormitory, wearing homespun unadorned uniform garments, eating simple fare, spending most of the time in silence, and contemplative meditation (McCarthy 1960).

For the most part, this life was open only to women of landed families. It included those who were offered for this kind of life by pious families who believed that having a relative in an order of consecrated virgins to pray for them and to sing God's praises would bless their families and their city. Some of those women were offered by families at the tender ages of six to ten. In such cases, the commitment was a family decision rather than a personal one. Although these members learned the discipline of the life in an atmosphere of kindness and community, subsequent opportunities to relax the rigors of the life were taken by some when they became available. This led, after a while, to some laxity in following the prescribed rule, resulting in serious disciplinary restrictions.

The development of the life of the monastery-convent was well underway in the sixth century when St. Caesarius, Bishop of Arles in southern France (then Gaul), provided the first complete religious rule, the shaping of which and its testing absorbed much of his interest between the years 512 and 534, when the final version was completed. He chose the first abbess, his own sister, and the entire religious community was accountable to him. Nevertheless, he had the vision to seek, by papal bull, the exemption of the convent from the control of his successors. He further assured that it had sufficient land and lay personnel to provide the nuns with adequate produce for years to come. In writing his rule, he had consulted the only earlier rule, that of St. Augustine, itself only a letter of advice probably written for a community of nuns in North Africa at the end of the fifth century. Although we have little knowledge about how the nuns received the rule of St. Caesarius, we do know that the convent prospered, increasing in membership from its first four members to over two hundred before his death (McCarthy).

Another trend in the monastic life for women was derived from the Benedictine tradition. The Benedictine rule, though created for men, was adopted and adapted by women.[5] This process of adaptation included the changes incorporated in the Cistercian reform, which modified the strict work and prayer cycle with a rich liturgical emphasis. The Benedictine and Cistercian monasteries of men, though they provided the monasteries of women with sacramental services, lay brother workers and legal aid regarding property, refused for centuries to recognize the women as belonging to the Benedictine Order. Although officially unrecognized, convents of Benedictine nuns spread all over Europe (Thompson 1978, p. 232). One can see the classic style of monastic life, as we know it today, emerge and develop through the succeeding centuries as autonomous Benedictine communities proliferated. These convents provided opportunities for single women to become well educated, to have influence in spiritual direction, and, in some cases, even a degree of power in the church (Power 1975, p. 99).

Nevertheless, almost every century included a flourishing and then a decline in this contemplative form of religious life. The exhortation to reform was sometimes strongly rejected by the members, even at times to the point of physically resisting the bishop and taking up arms against his warriors (Hilpisch 1950, p. 53). Inevitably, there were disputes leading to lawsuits against the abbots of nearby monasteries of men, responsible for the spiritual direction of the nuns and the care of their property (Boyd, p. 110ff).

The Decline and Fall

The eventual decline in the fervor with which the contemplative life was lived had several underlying causes, some constant, others varying. In each instance, the decline involved abbesses breaking the cloister by going out, often because of business relating to the convents. This was a necessary departure from custom since these were small, poorly endowed foundations, waning in membership. However, the records of decline also include other infractions of the rule: the wearing of elegant clothes and jewelry; introducing dancing; going to weddings; neglecting study; avoiding the common meals; sleeping through the divine office; shirking the common work and living in separate apartments with one's servants in attendance. The subsequent reforms always reintroduced a simple lifestyle, reactivation of the regular life, more attention to prayer and the introduction of works of mercy. Research suggests that sexual scandals and dissolute life, sometimes suggested, are, for the most part, wrongly assigned as the main elements of the corruption and eventual decline. The laxity consisted rather in the adoption of a more luxurious way of living (Power 1975, p. 98).

The Cloister

The problems arising from the presence of unwilling members climaxed in the year 1298 in the proclamation of a papal bull that imposed cloister on religious institutes of women, a restriction in force until the opening of the twentieth century. Again, there were structural as well as ascetic reasons for mandating this rule of enclosure. By the end of the thirteenth century, convents housed not only those seeking a contemplative life in praise of God but others also: those daughters of feudal lords for whom there were no dowries; unfaithful wives put away by their husbands; illegitimate offspring who could not inherit and were in need of shelter; and, after the Black Death, women who had lost their families and who paid to be cared for in the convents until death (Ewens 1978, p. 18). Around these pragmatic arrangements and charitable concerns, laxity reached such a point that Pope Boniface VIII issued a decree in 1298 entitled *Periculoso*. In part, it reads:

> Desiring to provide for the perilous and detestable state of certain nuns, who, having slackened the reins of decency have shamelessly cast aside the modesty of their sex, sometimes gad about outside their monasteries in the dwellings of secular persons and frequently admit suspected persons within the same monasteries, to the grave offence of Him

to Whom they have, of their own will, vowed their inno-
cence to the opprobrium of religion and to the scandal of
very many persons; we by the present constitution, which
shall be irrefragably valid, decree with healthful intent that
all and sundry nuns, present and future, to whatever order
they belong and in whatever part of the world, shall henceforth remain perpetually enclosed within their monasteries; so that no nun tacitly or expressly professed in religion
shall henceforth have or be able to have the power of going
out of those monasteries for whatsoever reason or cause,
unless perchance any be found manifestly suffering from a
disease so great and of such a nature that she cannot, without danger or scandal, live together with others; and to no
dishonest or even honest person shall entry or access be
given by them unless for a reasonable and manifest cause
and by a special license from the person to whom [granting
of such a license] pertains; that so, altogether withdrawn
from public and mundane sights, they may serve God
more freely and diligently preserve for Him in all holiness
their souls and their bodies. (Power 1922, p. 344).

This enclosure, called cloister, became so sacralized in practice that, through the years, women who banded together, even
six hundred years later, not for a contemplative vocation but for
common prayer and works of charity, were subjected to the
same rigid restrictions when they dedicated their lives to works
of human service in the local community (Ewens, p. 19). By the
year 1600, the keeping of the cloister had already come into conflict with the new call to women to serve the poor. Yet, it was
not until 1901 that any formal changes were made. Even 652
years after the promulgation of *Periculoso*, that is, in 1950, cloister remained as a central value not only for nuns but even for
sisters, although in 1950 the clear distinction of these two vocations, that of nun and sister, had been defined formally in *Sponsa
Christi* (Pius XII). This issue of the cloister, as we shall see, is critical to our analysis of modern congregations of sisters, particularly as it impinges on the question of the control of property

and the vow of poverty.

What characterized the life of early medieval nuns, as distinct from that of the sisters of today, was that the whole valued purpose of the dedicated life was fulfilled by prayer and praise of God. The community life, regular observance, cycle of work and study were introduced to help to make the prayer and praise effective. At the convent, education was provided, especially in the high Middle Ages, for a few select young women, children of the gentry, most of whom were expected to remain as religious members once they were old enough to make that choice. Although convent training did generate educated women, particularly before the decline of the late Middle Ages, education was not its primary function, nor was service to the poor and travelers who were fed at the door of the convent, though both of those functions were associated with convent life. The poor were cared for, if not at the monastery, then in the village, because if they became too noisy waiting at the convent door, serving their needs was removed to the village church lest it disturb the contemplation of the nuns (McCarthy). Today we call this secluded vocation of nuns in the church the contemplative life. It still attracts, as it did in those days, a small proportion of dedicated women (and men also), who live entirely apart from the stresses of what is defined as "the world." In the United States, at the present time, there are about 4000 contemplative nuns; but there are 106,000 active sisters. The callings are distinct, as we shall see, even though the church was slow in giving recognition to the differences.

Period II: 1600 to 1950

Beginning in the sixteenth century and accelerating into the twentieth, a new form of religious commitment of vowed women in the Catholic church emerged and became institutionalized. Women who attempted to combine the contemplative vocation with an active involvement in alleviation of the sufferings caused by poverty became semi-cloistered. Their effort to minister to human needs is as old as the church itself. Serving the poor, the sick and the illiterate was a priority in the original mandate of Christians. The Christian community always provided for some poor and some strangers in the local church. The call of consecrated women in the early industrial era, from about 1600 onward, was that of responding differently to human need. Theirs was a call to a more systematic form of alleviating the results of the poverty caused by the *laissez-faire* development of the early western industrial city. The women who answered this call expected to walk the streets and alleys of the city, to meet the poor there, as well as in their homes, hospitals and at work, and to do something effective to help them in their sufferings. Yet, the church still insisted on the imposition of the cloister.

The Cloister or Good Works

In the face of this tension, in 1544 Angela Merici, founder of the Ursuline order of nuns, envisioned an uncloistered order to teach and serve the poor. After a brief successful effort, however, she was forced by church authorities to reintroduce the cloister (Myers 1965, p. 10). Later, Jeanne de Chantal founded the Visitation nuns for ministry to the urban poor in the first decade of the seventeenth century. By 1615, however, the church hierarchy so insisted on cloister that she had to choose between establishing it or working with the poor with a non-religious affiliation for her group. She chose cloister. There were many more initiatives by women who saw the sufferings of the city poor as a new development demanding a new response. As in the earlier period, when insistence on the institution of marriage generated resistance to the celibacy initiative of women who did not wish to marry, now it was the institution of property which elicited opposition. A subtle relationship between the ownership of property and the vow of poverty developed as it became institutionalized in the later Middle Ages.

Poverty or Property

The women who chose these new apostolic callings to serve the poor frequently came from families of land owners who had many children to provide for. One way to accommodate their obligations was by the highly institutionalized protection afforded by the solemn vow of poverty taken by cloistered nuns which precluded their claim to ownership (Leyser 1979, p. 64). By the solemn vow of poverty, in imitation of the simplicity of life that characterized Jesus, nuns gave up their legal rights to own or inherit property forever. However, should the nuns, in the course of their ministry, come out of the cloister to serve the poor, they would require buildings and resources to house and feed those in need. Consequently, these nuns would be making demands on their families, towns and church, demands to which the social system was not ready to respond. Thus, those who gathered to pray and to serve were required by church discipline to choose between prayer and service. The founders of the Ursulines and the nuns of the Visitation chose cloister as the higher good. The theology of that time defined that choice as the more perfect way for those women seeking perfection (Ewens). It is not easy to see, beneath the surface of the institution of solemn vows, the pragmatic of protection of estates from inheritance claims, but it is there (Power 1922, 1975). What this pragmatic did was to obscure the quality of holiness in the new call and to stifle the urgency of that call. The resistance to the necessary structural change in the lives of nuns was powerful, as we shall see.

Daughters of Charity

In order to address the new and pressing need to minister to the poor in an urban setting, Vincent de Paul in 1633 suggested a new way of religious life to a group of women interested in founding a hospital. Led by Louise de Marillac, the Daughters of Charity were ready to give up the idea of being nuns and taking solemn vows, in order to respond to the needs of the sick poor as consecrated women in the city. Vincent's formula at that time was considered revolutionary:

> The sisters shall have no convent but a hospital, houses of the sick or an asylum, no cell but a hired room, no chapel but the parish church, no cloister but the streets of the town; for a grille the fear of God, for a veil, holy modesty.

(Letters of St. Vincent de Paul, referenced in current Constitutions of Daughters of Charity)

This elimination of the physical structures of convent, grille and habit, which the long tradition had defined as essential to protect the virtue of the consecrated virgin, was seen as so radical by the church authorities that these sisters were not allowed to make permanent vows but only yearly renewals. Their whole consecration was considered something less than the authentic consecrated life. Not until the year 1900, when Pope Leo XIII published the papal decree *Conditae a Christo* and the *Normae* to implement it, were these sisters (and the over 500 new congregations that had come into existence in the almost three hundred intervening years) recognized in the canons of the Catholic church as true religious congregations (Ewens, p. 20). Yet, despite these restrictions over a span of three hundred years, hundreds of congregations which provided human services had been founded and had flourished and worked within the church.

During the years from 1600 to 1900, strong pressures were exerted through canonical pronouncement to enforce the restrictions of cloister on the women trying to do effective service in society. The church insisted that they wear the veil and the religious dress (habit), which seemed to symbolize the semi-monastic calling. The religious habit, in its origins, was actually the garb of the peasants or of aristocrats of the time, depending on place of foundation. It was never intended to be distinctive or to become sacralized in its archaic form. The church further required: partial cloister, travel in pairs, recitation of the liturgical office in whole or in part, or some substitute form of it, and exact hours for common prayer. In the course of time, all these regulations focused the life once again on cloister and contemplation. Many women, however, came to value dearly the combined contemplative-active form of spirituality. To guide this semi-contemplative trend, definitions of value were incorporated into retreats, days of recollection and sermons, with an emphasis that equated non-conformity with infidelity to the vocation. In spite of this ambiguity, the groups of women who chose this way of active life multiplied. Most of these congregations sprang up in Europe, many in response to problems of the bourgeois revolutions that left in their wake many orphans and abandoned elderly, as well as unschooled village children.

A subtle problem presented itself when monasteries were outlawed in France and elsewhere on the continent and attempts were made to exert government control over properties. The nuns and monks were dispersed because their life of prayer was defined as useless by the new states. Many of them moved to America and to the other countries colonized by new European states. In their new pioneer locations, however, the religious were encouraged to do works of the apostolate to the poor and to provide education for Catholics at all levels. They were also responsible for their own support, since they were now without property. Their services were sorely needed in new dioceses which were also poor. Due to the exile-like quality of their lives, some in vows came to think of these works as part of the secular trend stemming from the French Revolution and its aftermath. The new secular states in Europe welcomed these services, even where they disapproved of the monastic life as such. The dichotomy, viewed by some, between life and work, between prayer and human service, set up tensions of priority within religious institutes between the prayer and the apostolic work commitments of the sisters. It also generated some suspicion of the call to active ministry as a purely human and, hence, secular interest. Sisters committed to this calling had to prove their religious spirit by giving external indication of their life of prayer, a further complication to this active-contemplative lifestyle.

Doers of Good Works

Although few of the accounts of the founding and spread of religious congregations of women have reached the public press, archives of these groups provide rich, if sometimes quaint, accounts of the struggles and initiative of these resourceful pioneer women. Simply citing the names and brief accounts of the activities of some of those founders and their related groups attest to the rich store of creative action that flourished, despite the restraints on the semi-active/contemplative vocation. For example, Jeanne Fontbonne joined the Sisters of St. Joseph at Lyons, France, in 1778. After resisting the demands of the government to take the civil oath during the revolution and having her execution stayed in 1794 by the fall of Robespierre, she refounded a congregation in 1808.[6] By 1938, these sisters had opened 244 convents with 3000 women in residence, all of whom were teaching in day schools and operating hospitals and orphanages, as well as boarding schools [SSJ, 1936]. In Germany, Francisca Hoell and Pauline Schmid founded a group which they called School Sisters of St Francis. Dispensed from vows because of Bismarck's *Kulturkampf*, they opted to regroup and come to the United States. By 1905, there were 590 members staffing 98 schools in the Wisconsin area alone (Rothluebber 1965). In 1800, Madeleine Sophie Barat, born in Burgundy, France, and of peasant background, founded the Religious of the Sacred Heart, another teaching congregation. Within her lifetime, her sisters settled in France, Italy, Germany, Canada, the United States, Chile, Cuba, Egypt and Japan. By 1965, they had established 111 foundations (Charmot 1953). The School Sisters of Notre Dame were founded in Bavaria by Caroline Gerhardinger. Although bishops tried to retain them in one diocese and to develop independent groups by diocese, she successfully resisted this form of organization. Within the first six years, 60 postulants joined her and she soon had houses in all seven dioceses of Bavaria and a foundation in the United States (Friess 1907). By 1879, the year of the death of their founder, there were 2500 School Sisters of Notre Dame in the world. Julie Billiart, a peasant woman from Picardy in France, founded in 1803 the Sisters of Notre Dame of Namur, with a co-founder, Francoise Blin de Bourdon. The latter, like Jeanne Fontbonne, escaped the guillotine with the death of Robespierre. This is another congregation founded to teach poor girls in post-revolutionary France, with the explicit intention of moving around the world, an intention carried out despite resistance from the bishop of the founding diocese of Amiens. By 1898, the Sisters of Notre Dame had opened 111 convents—51 in Belgium, 18 in England, 1 in Scotland, 38 in the United States and one each in South Africa and Rhodesia (now Zimbabwe) and the Belgian Congo (now Zaire). Many more were to follow, including foundations in Asia and later ministries in other African nations and in Latin America.

Other foundations began in North America. In Canada, Marguerite D'Youville, born in Quebec in 1701, founded the Grey Nuns to do whatever work was necessary to help the needy. By 1971, there were 7000 Grey Nuns in Canada and the United States. The enterprises she initiated to finance her congregation included selling beer and running a ferryboat (Fitts 1971). The Immaculate Heart Sisters of Monroe, Michigan, were founded in 1845 through the assistance of a French priest, Louis Florent Gillet, who worked with Marie Therese Maxis, Therese Renawld, and Charlotte Martha Shaaf to found a congregation for the education of youth. By 1944, they had 1,047 Sisters working in the Midwest, with another branch of several hundred working out of the Pennsylvania area (Sr. Rosalita). Mollie Rogers, born in Boston, founded the Maryknoll Missionary Sisters in 1919. By 1947, she had established houses in China, Korea, Hawaii, and the Philippines. It is from this group and the Ursulines that the three sisters murdered by the National Guard in El Salvador in 1980 were to come. These brief notes scarcely touch the astounding record of the over five hundred separate foundations of the thousands of women who chose this semi-monastic vocation in the nineteenth century.[7]

Period III: 1950 to the Present

By 1950, it had become clear that the demand for sisters to staff schools, hospitals, and welfare centers and to do missionary work all over the world far exceeded the outreach of the one million sisters then in religious congregations. There was an ever increasing need for trained professional competency in the fields of health, education and welfare work in which the sisters were engaged. Earlier, in 1929, Pope Pius XI, in an encyclical entitled *The Christian Education of Youth*, had announced that religious should receive the full credentialed education necessary to carry out these important tasks. Between the late 1920s and 1950, especially in the United States, where the demand for professional credentials was accelerating, sisters were obediently responding to those new expectations and often under trying conditions. During summers and on weekends, they were taking their university training. During the week, they were trying to fulfill the requirements of a prayer schedule that took a full three hours of time daily, along with their hospital, school, or other institutional commitments. Many were feeling the strain (Myers).

Pope Pius XII was concerned about the justice dimension of adequate training for sisters in the provision of the services they would render and the tensions involved in preparing for the many works in which they were to be engaged. Accordingly, when he called for a World Congress on the States of Perfection, held in Rome in 1950, the problems of religious formation, among other issues, were examined (Myers). A whole series of international and national meetings followed with the purpose of examining the stresses and structures of the various forms of the vowed life: a General Congress of Religious in 1950; an International Conference of Teaching Sisters in 1951; and an International Congress of "Mothers General" in 1952 (Ple, *et al.* 1961). Then, more specifically for the American situation, beginning in 1953, under the influence of those international assemblies, a series of Institutes on Spirituality were held at Notre Dame University. Each afforded instructions for heads of religious congregations and their formation personnel for the careful development of new members and the ongoing education of older members (Haley 1954). Out of these deliberations came the establishment of formal organizations of heads of congregations: the Conference of Major Superiors of Religious Congregations of Women (CMSW) and a corresponding one for men (CMSM) and, on the international level, the International Union of Superiors General (UISG). These groups began the more systematic examination of the whole question of prayer and good works. They did so in the context of the new conditions of a

modern post-war world, highly technologized and individualis-
tically oriented in the West, with a new consciousness of the developing cultures of mission lands, now called the Third World
nations.[8]

The Formation of Nuns and Sisters

No doubt stimulated by Pope Pius XII's expressed concerns, the
Sister Formation Conference was initiated in 1953 to develop a
professionally adequate and spiritually grounded pre-apostolic
education for new members. The Roman directives, promulgated by the Vatican Congregation for Religious, mandated the
modernization of religious garb and customs that had come to
give a too other-worldly character to sisters working in "the
world" (Ple 1950). The American leadership was emphasizing
professional competency for the services provided and an updated theological training as well. This combination of emphases introduced a slowly accelerating program of formation and
education that would culminate, at the time of the Second Vatican Council, with an almost entirely new conception of mission
and religious life.[9] This called for a vowed poverty not rooted in
the mere security of dependence, but rather opted for responsible stewardship, a sharing with those in need. It demanded a
celibate life for mission and a more responsible obedience to the
mission of the church as expressed in the gospels. The new challenge of a church mission of social transformation, rising out of
the development of peoples, sharpened the distinction between
nun and sister and promised to challenge the form of the third
vow, that of obedience.

Before we turn to the structural changes that set forth the new
focus on the vow of obedience, it is instructive to consider a significant papal document published in 1950: *Sponsa Christi*. In this
decree, Pope Pius XII, addressing nuns throughout the world,
discussed the question of how they earn their living. He noted
that the era of living on land gifts was past and that, in order to
continue to live the contemplative life in the modern world, they
would have to earn their living. He counseled nuns, therefore,
to do only those works that would not distract them from their

primary purpose of direct prayer and praise of God (Pius XII, 1950).

Nuns could recognize the wisdom of this advice and sisters could also recognize clearly that it did not apply to them. The sisters were encouraged by the document's distinction between their apostolic service to the needy, never to be treated as potential distractions from prayer, and the functional work nuns were recommended to do to provide for their living. Now, at last, the need for sisters to seek an apostolic spirituality consonant with their mission became clearer. With this clarification, sisters were released officially from the constraints of a lifestyle that had come to interfere with the quality of their service to human beings. The result was an ever clearer focusing on the search for a spirituality with a central concern to serve the neighbor in need and to do so in biblical perspective within the signs of the times. The signs of the times turned out to be a major challenge in the final decades of the twentieth century, particularly because of the discovery by the church of its own special option for the poor. This had an inevitable impact on the contemporary sister.

The Emergence of Modern Sisters

We now turn our attention, then, to religious women in the current era. By 1966, there were in the United States 181,000 sisters and nuns in over 500 different religious congregations and orders. The sisters were engaged in a variety of works: operating hospitals, orphanages, homes for the elderly, temporary shelters for homeless women, and working in special education for those with physical and mental disabilities, as well as in diocesan elementary and high school educational systems and college teaching (Neal 1984). In many cases, the sisters themselves had designed the buildings and run the fund-raising campaigns that provided for the 2,943 buildings in which they did their work, and 750 of which they owned and operated. The other centers were diocesan-owned, and, in some cases, diocesan-operated. At that time, 1966, teaching alone absorbed the labor of 66 percent of all the sisters in the United States.[10]

Most of the women who had answered this call to service in

the twentieth century were of working class background, a far cry from the aristocratic nuns of the Middle Ages. They still made out wills when they took their vows but few had any property to disown; few even had their college education upon entrance to religious life. Of those living and working in the United States in 1966, only 5 percent had entered with a degree. Only 20 percent had fathers whose occupation was classified as professional, and only 6 percent of their fathers and 3 percent of their mothers were college graduates. Yet, in 1967, 68 percent of the sisters themselves had at least a college education and by 1980 that number was 88 percent, with 68 percent having advanced degrees (Neal 1981, 1984).

The amazing increase in the religious vocations of women, to do service work in the church and to live a semi-contemplative life in community, reached its height in 1966 and then suffered a steep decline. It seems pertinent to note, however, that the increase in numbers of religious leaving congregations actually began in 1953, when systematic degree programs were introduced for all new members, as well as newly initiated theological programs based on the study of the most current theologians. In the late 1980s, although the upward trend of numbers leaving and downward trend in new members entering leveled off, the actual number of sisters is down 40 percent from 1966, and in 1983 new membership was but 15 percent of what it was in 1966. Furthermore, the age pyramid is vastly different, with 17.3 percent of the population over sixty-five in 1966, and 37.7 percent over that age in 1982. The under-forty group changed from 40 percent to about 16 percent in the same time span (Neal 1984).

Where have all the sisters gone? There are many theories and certainly more than one variable is involved. Some may argue that the very upgrading of sisters' professional training in the midst of the new women's movement offered so many more options for the women already in religious life and those considering religious life that the departure and non-entering trends are explained by that fact alone. However, this would not account for the earlier departures in the European countries nor the acceleration of entering trends in Third World countries. Furthermore, the opening of the church to lay women and men, eager to participate after the Second Vatican Council had recognized their baptismal calling to church work, certainly partially explains the trend. Another hypothesis suggests itself when one considers the radical risks implied in the new mission of the church to the poor. The old system had become like a tortoise's carapace, too rigid to respond effectively (Douglas 1972, p. 179). The congregations, sensing this limitation, reordered their priorities, reexamined their charisms, and rewrote their constitutions, the better to respond to the call to mission. Some groups of nuns and sisters have not yet heard the call; others hear it and find it alien to their present understanding of church; and still others find it too great a risk to respond immediately. The risk factor, adduced by this hypothesis, is, in fact, affecting membership at present.[11]

The new challenge which faces the church in the world since the early 1960s is that of the focus on the mission of human liberation. It is expressed in the church since the Second Vatican Council as "a special option for the poor." Chapter 2 will explain its origin and development. Here it is sufficient to say that the present research is designed both to study its effect on sisters and to measure its influence on religious congregational life in the United States up through the mid-eighties. The attempts of women religious to respond faithfully to this mission have challenged the traditional practice of obedience in religious congregations of women. Just as the origins of religious life in the church established the legitimacy of the vow of chastity, and the need for property challenged the solemn vow of poverty taken by contemplative nuns, so today the necessity for participatory decision making engages congregations committed to the new mission of solidarity with the struggles of Third World peoples. The obedience of sisters to the mission of the church sometimes comes into conflict with the very structure of the church, as these religious women stand with the poor reaching out to claim their rights to survive humanly. As they try to become responsible and accountable partners in decision making about the uses of God's creation, professionally trained women and men in the church find that the vow commitment to personal authority becomes a stumbling block. They must challenge historical structures of state and church that are primarily patriarchal. To do this, they seek to govern themselves in the model the church proclaims for the poor: to participate in the decisions that affect their own lives.

Critical Social Analysis

As noted above, prior to 1950, the church had defined commitment to mission, for both sisters and nuns, as secondary to their primary call to personal holiness (Ple, *et al.* 1961, p. 34). This focus long remained central, even though the principal intent of the apostolic congregations was to work among the poor. As the sisters' education became more systematic, they learned to reflect on the social conditions they witnessed. This reflection turned to critical analysis, as theology and education developed together. The socially concerned theologians of the fifties: Congar, de Lubac, Henri Chenu, Danielou, Karl and Hugo Rahner, Teilhard, and others who later became the periti at the Second Vatican Council (Neal 1965), alerted the sisters to the liberation movements that would be formalized by efforts in Third World nations. Missionaries, who brought news of these struggles and the foment of the civil rights movement in the United States, expanded commitment to human rights. Through their mission among the poor, some sisters developed a deepened understanding of the exploitation suffered by people who are without resources, and who are sick, uneducated and old. Their reflection on this oppression, clarified by the theological training afforded them in the 1950s, raised questions about services rendered without critical social analysis of the relationship between intention and outcome. The new questioning was reinforced by the documents of Vatican II which provide a major transition in the understanding of the relationships between religion and society. This new council understanding was articulated with growing clarity in the social encyclicals from 1891 through 1981. It was presented in Pope John XXIII's *Peace on Earth* (1963); and

Pope Paul VI's *The Development of Peoples* (1967), *Call to Action* (1971), and the implementing synod document of the same year: *Justice in the World*. All of these documents moved sisters to new insights about mission and vows. As they reviewed their constitutions, mandated for updating by the Second Vatican Council's *Decree on the Renewal of Religious Life* (Flannery 1975), many came to focus that review on the quality of their service to the poor (Neal 1984).

Pope Paul VI, in his exhortation to sisters for renewal, *Evangelica Testificatio* (1973), referred directly to his earlier *Call to Action* document and asked: "How can the call of the poor find an echo in the lives of religious?" (Section 18. See also Neal in LCWR, 1974). By 1980, this question was the dominant one in the renewal chapters of many religious congregations of women (see Chapter 3).

The resultant growing awareness that health, education and subsistence services are finally being recognized as human rights, to be provided for by common wealth and global resources, explains the new concern of sisters to share in transforming work with poor people. They wish to work with their lay professional colleagues and to join ecumenically with Christians and other groups to further the church's mission to the liberation of Third World peoples (Neal 1981). As a result of this shift of emphasis, many women's congregations have changed their lifestyles and reworked their own statements of mission in line with the stated new directions of the church's mission. Their statements now describe their mission, therefore, in these general terms: a call to biblically-grounded action for the transformation of the unjust structures of modern society in privileged and underprivileged nations. In this era, new members do not look to the congregations for a commitment to being "spouses of Christ," which is the nun's vocation (*Sponsa Christi*), nor for the security of a stable community life. They do so, rather, for their obedience to the call to fulfill the newly specified and more clearly articulated mission of the church: the transformation of societal structures of injustice. It is a commitment to finding God in the cries of the poor as they seek to organize themselves and assert their rights as human beings. It is a commitment, on the part of the non-poor, to respond to the just demands of the poor. It is a discovery of a new theology worked out in action and reflection, as deeply contemplative as the earlier spiritualities but now re-routed to action in response to the signs of the times. [12] It includes identification with the poor of the world who have begun to hear their own call from God to claim the land in order to feed their children. This agenda, the central concern of the church only since the Second Vatican Council, challenges old traditions still rooted in a patriarchal model. Such an anachronistic model defies solutions of some of the problems of the world's peoples because its institutions are entirely inadequate to plan for and to address new needs. This newer position even considers the institution of war, utilized and rationalized as a way to resolve human conflicts, as outmoded. These are the problems sisters are addressing today.

Obedience to the Mission of the Church

Possible solutions for the problems of the dispossessed are proffered in the theses of liberation theology, developed in a setting of biblical reflection on the claims of the poor to the resources of the land, whether it be for housing in the city or self-determination in Third World settings.[13] They are also expressed in the mission statements of revised constitutions of many religious congregations of Catholic sisters. As the sisters meet in chapter and revise their constitutions, they listen to each other, often with greater attention than in the past, thoughtfully reflecting on the experiences of their sisters and brothers in places characterized by a poverty that could be eliminated, were the power centers of the world not absorbed in a different agenda.[14] Chapter 3 will discuss these constitutions and the roots of their uniqueness.

Through this study of constitutions, we will see that the transformation of the sisterhoods was, in each instance, the way by which members attempted to revitalize the life of the church, in which the elimination of the causes of poverty now takes precedence over alleviating its results. It is social organization, at present, that prevents the effective implementation of the mission of the church. The understanding and free creativity needed to solve problems of human need are not to be gained in a cumbersome and omniscient patriarchal structure, historically outdated (Lerner 1986). As has been the case throughout history, radical changes in the structure of the lives of women in the vowed life in the church are largely radical responses to secular institutions that no longer promote the survival and well-being of all peoples. In the time of Christ and in the early years of Christianity, a transition was needed to allow some women to be free from family responsibilities to live a single life of prayer and service. Later, in feudal times, changes in inheritance laws unmasked some of the self-serving functions to which cloister had been put and made possible a more mobile urban life for women seeking to minister to the poor. Similarly today, development in the understanding of the vow of obedience has sought changes essential to shift the church's emphasis. The focus has moved from the sometimes unquestioning obedience to another person—who alone cannot have sufficient expertise to make decisions for the group—to obedience to a Gospel mandate that affirms both the full participation of all people in the decisions that affect their lives and their accountability for the chosen outcomes.[15] Unexamined obedience and patriarchy have revealed their own ineffectiveness. The world's peoples, who have spoken out for social justice, have revealed the new direction of the vowed life.

So it is that, although sisters perceive what needs to be done in their ministries of apostolic service, they are often restrained by conserving traditional structures of a patriarchy, a system which seeks to use the traditional family model of relationships—parent to child. Evidence is accumulating that many sisters today are increasingly caught in a dilemma of, on the one hand, obedience to the stated mission of the church and the mandated initiative to carry it out; and on the other, a sacralized mandate of obedience to the authority of a person whose will takes precedence even over the doing of this mission. At this writing, it would seem that the vow of obedience is facing the same challenges experienced by the vow of celibacy in the early church and the vow of poverty at the beginning of the seventeenth century. What forms the transformation will take, however, are not yet clearly articulated, even though they are already being shaped in our own historical milieu. We turn now, in the next chapter, to take a closer look at the mission of the church of the 1980s as it encompasses the particular vocation of sisters.

—2—

Prophetic Ministry and Risk

In the fall of 1980, four church women died in El Salvador. Although they have already been cited in the previous chapter, their names bear repeating here: Maura Clark, Ita Ford, Dorothy Kazel, and Jean Donovan. The first three were American sisters; the fourth, an American lay volunteer who worked with them. They were engaged in doing what, in the nineteenth century, began to be called missionary work. But their lives and their work in El Salvador were not in the old traditional mold. In their mode of presence and in their ministry, these women identified more closely with the people among whom they served than with the policies of the governments of either El Salvador or of the United States, the latter their country of origin. They were helping the poor exercise their claim to the land they had tilled for centuries (Neal 1987; John Paul II 1988). They were teaching religion, witnessing to a simple lifestyle, celebrating Eucharist with the local clergy and people, praying in Christian communities, helping to feed, clothe, shelter and heal the poorest. But they were also reflecting with them on their rights to the land. They were raped and killed by the National Guard. What actually did happen is still a government secret, though the facts are known *not* to be what was suggested on subsequent television newscasts: that they were Communist accomplices.[1] They were doing a prophetic ministry; in so doing, they risked their lives unto death. In letters written but a short time before their deaths, they spoke of risk of death. So too had the sermons of Archbishop Oscar Romero, the head of the diocese in which these killings occurred, spoken of death; he had been murdered while celebrating the liturgy in a convent chapel a few months previously. How did the church so influence the work of the sisters and that of others working in the interests of the poor?

One Hundred Years of Vatican Teaching

Beginning in the late nineteenth century, the Catholic church, through papal documents, sponsored a series of anniversary papal encyclicals that addressed the condition of the workers in industry and of the farmers on the land. Responding in large part to the challenge of agrarian and urban socialists' claims that the church was identifying with the elite and neglecting the plight of the poor, Pope Leo XIII published in 1891 *Rerum Novarum*, entitled in English *On the Conditions of the Working Class*. This, the first of the social encyclicals, affirmed the right of workers to a fair share of the profits of industry, sufficient to live in simple dignity with their families (Leo XIII). Its rationale was derived from biblical and historical sources. In 1931, Pope Pius XI, in *Quadragesimo Anno*, developed this thesis further and supported the rights of workers to organize and to use the strike and the boycott to increase their bargaining power with management (Pius XI). In 1961, Pope John XXIII in *Mater et Magistra*, in English *Christianity and Social Progress*, called the Latin American church to account for its alignment with the power of the state and the wealth of industry, and urged its affiliation with the struggling workers and farmers instead. Pope Paul VI's *Octogesima Adveniens* (*Call to Action*), appeared in 1971. This encyclical invited all committed Christians to transform the structures of their society through political action and according to principles of social justice and peace. This invitation was issued because, as the document noted, since transnational corporations were no longer under the control of any sovereign state, all committed Christians were called to enter political action to transform unjust social structures in accord with principles of justice and peace.

The sequence continued into 1981 when Pope John Paul II published *Laborem Exercens*, stressing the priority of labor over capital and indicating that the rights of ownership to the means of production stem from the labor of the workers through the centuries. However, leading up to these strong conclusions of *Laborem Exercens* were the papal statements of the previous decade which developed in depth, with powerful scriptural and historical linkages, a strong affirmation of the growing awareness of the rights of peoples to share fully in the development of resources for life. In 1963, Pope John XXIII published *Pacem in Terris*, claiming that peace, poverty and human rights are the central concerns of the committed Christian. After this document came the call to Vatican II. Among the most influential documents of the council was the *Pastoral Constitution of the Church in the Modern World*, which invited Christians to review their customs and traditions in order to purge them of sinful structures, that is, of rules that brought death rather than life to suffering multitudes. Shortly after the council, in 1967, Pope Paul VI promulgated *Populorum Progressio*, which supported the rights of peoples to self-determination and encouraged all church members to participate in this development. In 1971, following *Call to Action*, the bishops of the world were summoned to a Synod in Rome. This Synod had for its purpose the implementation of the *Call to Action* and, to that end, produced a document entitled: *Justice in the World*. This document expressed the clearest statement of the new direction of the church's option for the poor. The famous words are these:

> Action on behalf of justice and participation in the transformation of the world fully appear to us as a constitutive dimension of the preaching of the Gospel or in other words of the church's mission for the redemption of the human race and its liberation from every oppressive situation. [2]

The Office of Justice and Peace

This document initiated the establishment of Justice and Peace

Offices that now exist in most dioceses of the world and in most religious congregations of women and men. From these centers come the initiatives for action to eliminate poverty, racism, class oppression, and sexism, and to participate in anti-war activities that now characterize so many local churches, especially those attached to parishes where the poor are learning how to change the oppressive conditions of their own lives. Out of this bishops' synod came the Call to Action Conference of the Catholic church in the United States in the bicentennial year, 1976. From that Conference developed the plans for the Bishops' pastorals on racism (1979), Hispanics (1983), peace (1983), the economy (1986), and the pastoral on women (1988). (See United States Catholic Conference of Bishops in the bibliography.)

Social Sin

Finally, to complete this saga of social concern in ecclesial perspective, in early 1988 Pope John Paul II issued the encyclical *Sollicitudo Rei Socialis* (On Social Concerns). Biblical and historical references linked this document directly to *Populorum Progressio*, published two decades earlier, which indicated that the option for the poor would take priority as the active form of working to eliminate the causes of poverty, though not to the neglect of traditional works of charity and healing. This post-Vatican II era of church emphasis on involvement in the transformation of the world is related to the origins of Liberation Theology, which was, in 1968, taking form out of the lived experiences of Base Christian Communities in Latin America (Gutiérrez 1988). *Sollicitudo Rei Socialis* names as "sinful structures" aspects of both liberal capitalism and Marxist collectivism, as they confront each other in two powerful global blocs and prevent the development of poor peoples while enhancing the wealth of a few. It also indicates whose responsibility it is to change these unjust conditions by indicating that private property "has a social mortgage." This document formally links the global situation of 1988 with the development of peoples, also encouraged in *Populorum Progressio* in 1967. That too was the year of the first initiative of Latin American bishops, at their Medellin Conference, responding to the Base Christian Communities and the beginnings of the new liberation theologies for which Latin America has become world-known. The Puebla Conference of the same bishops, ten years later in Mexico, despite some opposition, furthered this type of theological reflection at the grassroots level in Base Christian Communities (see Berryman 1984, 1987).

This theological activity in the local churches of Latin America has had worldwide influence on not only the restructuring of the religious life of Catholic sisters in their role as missionaries, but also indigenous new congregational members who attended the renewal Chapters. Much impetus came from the accounts of delegates from the mission lands who reported to the sisters from First World countries. They reflected with them about the meaning of this new biblical life in the church where the people were learning literacy by examining the injustices of their local situations and hence raising their political consciousness. But media programmers are also members of these local communities and are formed by that membership. The media channels for shaping point of view affect the whole educational endeavor, more particularly religion and family socialization. Publically and privately sponsored television, radio, and journals of information powerfully influence viewers, listeners and readers.

Although wealth and power groups often control and sponsor media, social ideologies are closely linked to class interests, and hence to education. Such documents as social encyclicals, promulgated by official church bodies, can become extremely influential if they are heeded and thoughtfully incorporated into church teaching, pastoral action and programs for formation for mission.

Although the encyclicals have not always been so treated, they were studied seriously in the decade of the economic depression (1930s) and again in the post-1960 era. Fortuitously or sacramentally—it is not easy to ascertain degrees of each possibility—the renewal of religious congregations of women focused on commitment to mission at the very time that the importance of these documents was alive in the awareness of the post-Vatican church. As a result, the sisters were newly open to

linking the original charism of their congregations with the current mission of the church. Missionaries, particularly, became
sensitive to the application of the council directives to the pover-
ty-stricken areas of Latin America, Asia and Africa, where they
were living their vocations in post-colonial and newly imperial-
ist settings. It is true that Marx's critique of the entrenched cultures that justified the exploitation of workers did address the
inhumane realities and injustice of their situations. So did his
critique of religion as the opium of the people. But the justice
themes adopted in response to these prophetic denunciations
came directly out of the life of the church, especially as it was
expressed in the poor rural areas of Third World countries (see,
for example, Cardenal 1976). Labelling the responses of some religious as "Marxist" was politically strategic, perhaps, to resist
change inimical to the self-interests of the advantaged but it was
also analytically naive (Neal 1972).

The action of the church, choosing to dissociate itself in 1961
from established political and economic interests, was considered an alarming development for some, particularly those who
considered change, transformation and the destabilization of the
socio-economic status quo to be Marxist-oriented. The seeming
link of this new movement for justice with Marxism, however,
resided more in the social analysis characteristic of both orienta-
tions than in an explicit and shared planning for change (Adriance 1986; Gallo 1988). Urban sociologists and sociologists of religion had clearly pointed to the uses of Christianity by the
colonialists to develop a politically uncritical and cooperative
workforce in Africa, Asia, and Latin America. Marx noted this
link in the nineteenth century and neo-Marxists could still find
evidence of it in the twentieth century. Marx's critique of religion as "the opiate of the people" was substantiated in the content of many sermons preached to the people. Many of the very
poor were asked to be patient with their lot in life and to wait
for heaven for their reward. Sermons to the workers urged them
to be industrious, frugal and obedient in the workplace, and
promised them heaven for their disciplined life. The advantaged
were recommended to thank God for showering blessings upon

them, undeserving though they might be. As Max Weber pointed out in the early twentieth century, such sermons subvert the
just revolution. They assure an uncritical work force and an unaware "kept" class of more advantaged middle management people. At the same time, they leave the conscience of the advantaged free of any sense that their way of life impinges on the
struggle of the very poor, often preventing the achievement of
their basic human rights to life (Weber 1922).

Eventually, however, the concerted and sometimes orches-
trated efforts of established cultural institutions to prevent or
delay change began to falter. This happened when, in the second half of the twentieth century, the socio-politico-economic
systems, which not only subjugated the poor but maintained the
notion of poverty as a viable destiny for many, increasingly became objects of criticism and social protest. Organized for discussion and biblical reflection, in missionary settings and often
in the environments of Base Christian Communities, many in
Latin America, Asia and Africa came to perceive the functional
links between their poverty and the unwillingness of elites to
eliminate it. In these religiously-oriented contexts, they meditated on this relationship and on other factors causal to their economic deprivation. Several critical facts became particularly evident to them: that the resources of the world are adequately
sufficient for all to share; that those resources are unjustly distributed; that the past and continuing non-participation of the
poor in the planning for production and/or for distribution of
the earth's resources perpetuated existing inequities, and, most
significantly, blocked access for many people to the means of
their survival (Gutiérrez; Berryman).

From Radical Critique to Church Mandate

In reversal of its admonitions of peace, order and submission at
all costs, the church has had considerable positive influence in
this process of consciousness-raising. Much of the twentieth-
century missionary work has participated in Third World peoples' coming alive to the Good News: that the land belongs to
them; that the people have not only the right but the obligation

to claim, work and harvest it, and to use it for life and not for death (Pope John XXIII, *Pacem in Terris*).[3] Moved by the experiences of their members, missionary societies of several denominations met in New Jersey in May 1983. They affirmed these conclusions of Good News for the poor and further agreed that the principal centers of Christianity have moved to Africa, Asia, and Latin America (*New York Times*, May 10, 1982, p. B6).

What are the implications of these conclusions and what are their corollaries in the responses of the church? One may grapple with these questions by observing the attitudes and actions of the churches with regard to the problem of the racism and injustice legally in place in South Africa. Churches protest the apartheid policy of South Africa because it represents a classic case of a continuing colonial insensitivity to human rights, a situation rejected by caring Christians and humanists of social responsibility.[4] Changes in basic social relations are major factors that ultimately move church people into social action for justice and peace. Today, that basic change lies both in the size and distribution of the world's population and in the modes of production and of distribution of the resources needed to provide for it. This calls the churches to a new way of doing "mission." For Christians, this means a call to share in the struggle of new generations of indigenous and migrant peoples as they seek leadership roles.

For some in the First World, false assumptions about insufficient food supplies and of other resources often generate hesitation to welcome migrants even to membership in their churches. There is such a long history that equates religious inclusion with nationalities that "old" immigrants forget sometimes that, going back a hundred years, their forebears were the "new" immigrants. Yet despite the reluctance of some members to accept the positive value of liberative change in the Third World, the church has committed itself to the future of these peoples. In renewing itself, the church has had to struggle against the resistance of its older ethnic members to share resources and power with younger churches. In doing so, church documents of the Second Vatican Council and bishops' pastorals expand these themes of social justice. The selfish church is also the altruistic church, a reality clearly expressed in church documents and in the spirit of those who accept them.[5]

Formation for a Justice Mission

A new mission, however, demands intense preparation and re-training. The kind of spiritual formation needed to prepare sisters well for this kind of service and for the missionary activity mandated by the social teachings of the church has been the subject of Catholic sisters' renewal activity since about 1963, particularly after the publication of *Pacem in Terris* (Cussianovich 1979; Dorr 1983). But it has been especially emphasized since the promulgation of the *Decree on Renewal of Religious Life*, a Second Vatican Council document of 1965. Having implemented carefully planned responses to this decree, sisters are now no longer merely reaching out to poor people to link them to their traditional works. They are, rather, helping whole nations of peoples to attain full recognition as peers with their fellow nations, and they are also assisting people within nation states toward a fuller self-development. The 16 documents of Vatican II, as well as Pope John XXIII's *Pacem in Terris* and Pope Paul VI's *Development of Peoples* encyclicals, put this mission, that of societal transformation, at the heart of their programs of spiritual formation (Flannery 1975). As cited above, the *Justice in the World* Synod document of 1971 announced these actions as "constitutive dimensions of the preaching of the gospel" (6). In reviewing the relevancy of their founding charisms, Catholic women in the vowed life have indeed taken seriously the new justice agenda of Christianity, now closer to ancient Judaism in its emphasis on the just possession of the land by the people (Leviticus 25).

Because the renewal of religious life in congregations of Catholic women became so closely linked with this new life of the church through the Second Vatican Council documents and the subsequent social justice directives, the work of the sisters on their constitutions focused, as we will soon see, on the implementation of the new agenda calling for a critical social analysis of existing political, economic and social systems, including, as *Mater et Magistra* so well expressed, even the structures of the church itself.

For Mary Douglas, an English anthropologist, the symbol of a tortoise shedding its carapace offers an apt analogy to describe processes of structural change. She likens the discarding of an antiquated and rigidly inflexible worldview for one truer to the times and functionally more relevant for the future, to the tortoise's inner mechanisms periodically releasing it from the restraints of its outgrown shell. This results in a new openness to life and possibility for renewed growth (Douglas 1972, p. 179). Women religious in the second half of the twentieth century have risked themselves as catalytic and creative agents for social change, in the interests of the silent and suffering poor, and in colleagueship with the organizing poor. In order to do so faithfully, they have struggled against the bonds of the carapace— the antiquated aspects of their society, their communities and their own lives. It is a struggle that still continues (Evans et al., Chapter 8).

Why is it that women, in the mid- and late-twentieth century, have taken up the difficult mission of furthering the liberation of peoples even at the risk of life? Edward Schillebeeckx, writing in 1979, one year before the murder of Archbishop Oscar Romero of El Salvador, could say with certainty that the doing of the mission of the church, as now designed, names death as one real risk because the mission calls for restoring the land to the people, an act obviously unacceptable to many. The Second Vatican Council mandated preparation for carrying out this mission, in men's and women's institutes alike, through study, reflection and action for justice.

The Call to Mission

The move to critical social analysis in the interests of structural change was manifest *earlier* in the formation programs of women's institutes in the United States than in men's.[6] The reason for this is that women undertook renewal in an all-encompassing and systematic way, which involved the entire membership, even worldwide in the case of international congregations. They deliberated about renewal, recorded points of view in opinion surveys and used the findings as starting-points for study and self-education. These data grounded the constitutional revisions, along with the decrees of the council and the subsequent document, *Justice in the World*. Today, as those revised constitutions come to the Congregation for Institutes of Consecrated Life to receive final approbation, it is the women's documents that express radical new directions toward societal transformation. The commitment to the mission of doing social justice in the world is clear and unambiguous in many of them. This is also true for some orders of men. However, women have also embodied these values and support for this new mission in organizational structures. These new structures include: government and community *for* mission rather than as ends in themselves; authority in the membership; and clear formulations about the object of the vows in the light of the church's special option for the poor (see Chapters 4 and 5).

But the external obstacles and difficulties remain manifold. The sisters find themselves in the dilemma of trying to fulfill their worldwide commitment to social transformation in an era of multi-faceted violence: nuclear stockpiling and the deployment of life- destroying weapons; racism, including that which recognizes an apartheid government as a Christian society; sexism, still reluctant to see women as equals, even within the church itself; and artificially created scarcity used to legitimate actions of national self-interest against the human rights of whole peoples. This is no longer the narrow and naive national politics of earlier generations. Today, sisters experience a self-conscious struggle of states against peoples. In an era of sophisticated technology, which should minimize mismanagement and expand the possibilities for full and open communication, manipulation often persists as the powerful try to control the transmission of necessary information and hence curb responsible action. In response, sisters' mission of education now seeks to incorporate an analysis of the function of symbolic manipulation by the various forms of media, ranging from text books to television. At a time when group altruism is needed to share resources for healing body and spirit, and for supporting life and human development, the denial of the potential of religion as a transforming energy in an unjust society is common. The vocation to respond to human need calls sisters to devise an education, therefore, that releases the Christian message from the unreflective consciousness of the advantaged, wherein symbol systems are so manipulated that they look religious, sound religious, and yet sometimes are destructive (Richard 1983). Committed by vow to peace, community-building and development, sisters find themseves compelled to take sides with the oppressed, which means that, sometimes, they are even in opposition to some of their colleagues within their own religious groups.

It is true that all sisters do not feel equally called to take radical risks. What their revised constitutions show, however, is that, as congregations, they are willing to be the communities of support for those who do take those risks for justice's sake. Further, they recognize that this mission of social transformation informs their ministry in the church, wherever they live and work, as an integral part of their vowed commitment. Their efforts have revealed the potential of institutionalized altruism for providing, in religious perspective, a more stable response to human needs (see Neal 1982). Clearly, the tensions at the present time center on incorporating this vision of a just society into formal congregational structures, within which old and new members alike commit themselves to a vowed life in a renewing church. More is needed, however. Institutional altruism, in order to be consistently and successfully directed, demands the establishment of formal norms of unselfish love for the other, devoid of motives of self-interest, of gaining profit or gratitude. In religious congregations, these include: the formulation of an explicit statement of mission; the development of a structure of government appropriate to that mission; and a lifestyle to witness to it. This formal structure then offers guidelines for choice of ministry, religious formation, apostolic spirituality and corporate commitments, all consonant with the founders' original charisms, and updated in an ecclesial context to respond more adequately to the signs of the times. In the next chapter, we will look at the content of some of these statements of mission, found in the revised constitutions of a variety of religious congregations of Catholic women.

— 3 —

Constitutions and Mission

On October 28, 1965, the *Decree on the Renewal of Religious Life* was produced, one of the 16 documents which came from the Second Vatican Council. It formalized an initiative in religious congregations of review and renewal that would radically change the way women would live the unique calling of consecrated apostolic religious life in the church. Its import was related closely to that of the other council documents, which embodied a complete updating of the Catholic church in the modern world. These documents stimulated what Pope John XXIII, in calling for the council in 1962, had labeled an *aggiornamento*. Every structure and function of the church was subjected to the scrutiny of the assembled bishops, some of whom had arrived well prepared with proposals for renewal from their local churches. Besides the document on the renewal of religious institutes, they produced others on diverse topics: the constitution of the church itself; the sacred liturgy; pastoral presence in the world; office of bishops; the ministry; life and training of priests; Christian education; relationships with other Christian and non-Christian religions; the apostolate of the laity; missionary activity; social communication; religious liberty and the relationship of the church with the modern world (Flannery 1975).

Guidelines for Renewal

The decree on religious life called for the most complete renewal ever undertaken of existing structures of religious life. It described religious life as "the pursuit of perfect charity" through "the practice of the evangelical counsels" (Matthew 8:20 and Luke 9:58) "in a communal life that is virginal, poor, and obedient." It set down principles for updating the manner of life that had become institutionalized over the centuries through custom and mandate. Each religious institute was invited to review its reasons for existing, and, in so doing, to examine both Scripture, and the intention of the founders, as a preparation for the revision of its constitutions and the subsequent modification of the lifestyle of its members.[1] One paragraph of the decree listed all that was to be re-examined and why:

> The manner of life of prayer and of work should be in harmony with present-day physical and psychological conditions of the members. It should also be in harmony with the needs of the apostolate in the measure that the nature of each institute requires, with the requirements of culture and with social and economic circumstances. This should be the case everywhere, but especially in mission territories. The mode of government of the institutes should also be examined according to the same criteria. For this reason, constitutions, directories, books of customs, of prayers, of ceremonies and such like should be properly revised, obsolete prescriptions being suppressed and should be brought in line with conciliar documents (Flannery, p. 613).

For reasons that we will examine later, it seemed, then, that the council intended the renewal of religious life to play a special role in the renewal of the church. Subsequent documents reinforced the mandate to renewal. A year after the first decree, a special apostolic letter was issued in August, *Ecclesiae Sanctae*, which contained further directives toward this renewal. Again, in June 1971 came Pope Paul VI's apostolic exhortation *Evangelica Testificatio (On the Renewal of the Religious Life According to the*

Teaching of the Second Vatican Council). Later, in 1983, Pope John Paul II also wrote an apostolic exhortation: *Redemptionis Donum* (*To Men and Women Religious on Their Consecration in the Light of the Mystery of the Redemption*).

All of these documents express a special interest in the way of life called "religious."[2] After the Vatican Council the way of the vowed life, with its centuries of invention, institutionalization and modification, was being called to witness and action in a special way. Paul VI asked of religious in *Evangelica Testificatio*:

> How then will the cry of the poor find an echo in your lives? That cry must, first of all, bar you from whatever would be a compromise with any form of social injustice. It obliges you also to awaken consciences to the drama of misery and to the demands of social justice made by the Gospel and the church (18).

This suggests that, as a result of the council, the church was defining itself in explicitly new ways which bespoke a heightened social awareness. In realizing its new direction, it was seeking help from those committed members who had chosen a form of consecration distinguished by the three vows of chastity, poverty and obedience.

Ecclesiologists, in studying the documents of Vatican II, concur that the church did set itself a new course at that time. Major characteristics of this new course are described in the two constitutions *Lumen Gentium* and *Gaudium et Spes*. The former, the *Dogmatic Constitution on the Church*, is the more basic one; the latter, the *Pastoral Constitution on the Church in the Modern World*, a guideline for action.[3] The fundamental theological shift introduced by these documents projected the church not as a Roman church but as a world church, a church for all peoples. Accordingly, it adopted the vernacular language of each local church and began to become indigenous by the ordaining of bishops from each local area. It announced the salvation of all peoples, irrespective of specific church affiliation.[4] By calling the church to action in the world, the Vatican Council in effect mandated a mission of human liberation, formalized in the already cited Justice in the World Synod of 1971 (see *Pastoral Constitution of the Church in the Modern World*, Chapter 2 in Flannery). The new perspective of church as "the people of God" assumed dominance over the concept of church as a formal structure, made up of an hierarchically-ordered community of clerics, religious, and laity. When the church administration invited religious to review their structures of government, it was, perhaps, even only subconsciously, also inviting models for its own future structure to serve the mission which it adopted in 1967 with the publication of *Populorum Progressio* (Pope Paul VI).[5]

Early Beginnings of Renewal

In retrospect, it is clear today that, as women in religious institutes went about the mandated tasks of renewal, they became aware of the implications of these broader church mandates to their mission in the church. In their own growing self-understanding and their increasing professional competency, they began to see the clear link between general church renewal and the updating of their own constitutions. However, what was unique to the renewal of congregations of sisters in the United States, as distinct from that of all other groups in the church, was the early element of planning for change. The history of this movement may seem, initially, to have been episodically haphazard. But this it never was. It is a story, rather, of action rich in theological inquiry and research, in reflective prayer and discourse, and in faithful sensitivity to the dignity of the human person. To this end, the actors in this story were ever attentive to how best to facilitate the personal and professional development of women and men religious. Some of these—in their psyches, lives and roles—were already in an undefined process of transformation; others would soon follow. Formally initiated by the Sister Formation Movement in 1951, deliberations and planning for change in religious congregations were well underway, when, in the summer of 1964, sixty men and women, already active in church renewal, were invited to the Grail in Loveland, Ohio, for a week of study of the church. This meeting was a spontaneous grassroots initiative. There, for a period of seven days, ten priests, ten sisters and forty other Catholic men and women met to study the changes in the church already indicated by preliminary drafts of council documents.[6] One of those drafts was the *Decree on Renewal of Religious Life*. Among those present were Sister Mary Luke Tobin, then president of the Conference of Major Superiors of Women (CMSW), and Sister Mary Daniel Turner, a member of the administrative board. They provided a direct channel for future planning. I was also a participant.[7] Urged by Denis Geaney, an Augustinian priest, we met to deliberate the impact of the renewal decree on sisters everywhere. As a result of their discussion, the sisters present decided to write a book about the pending changes. The following June (1965) the book was published. It was titled: *The Changing Sister* (Muckenhirn 1965, editor). Although it was rushed to publication, with editorial flaws uncorrected, it still had considerable impact because of its relevancy. The nine sisters whose articles were included in this publication had advanced degrees in various disciplines related to renewal: theology, philosophy, sociology, psychology, education, art, social work, and literature. The CMSW invited the writers to speak at their national meeting in September 1965.[8]

The Sisters' Survey

When the 28-member board of the CMSW met, they voted to do a systematic survey of the readiness for change among religious congregations. From their combined experience, they realized that there was a vast range of differences in the preparation of their many member groups for the changes expected of them, and that these differences should determine sound planning. The elements of the research design for the survey have already been reviewed (see Introduction and Note 9, Chapter 1). It is important to observe here that the survey's framework was adapted from the documents of the Council. Thus, from the very beginning of the renewal, those who worked on the study planned that the council documents would play a major role in setting the agenda and direction of renewal in women's religious institutes. Themes from the council were not only embodied in the survey's systematic data, but were later built into chapter deliberations after the results of the comprehensive Sisters' Survey had been examined.

Even by October 1966, when the special *Normae* was published, urging religious congregations to renewal, 437 institutes of women already had a considerable data base from the first report that compared their own congregations with the national profile of other congregations. This allowed them to determine the actual conditions of their group in the light of the council mandates (Neal 1984). Then by the fall of 1967, they also had a population profile of 139, 691 cases to compare with their own institute's scores on the Sisters' Survey. This second instrument had been sent to the entire membership of all congregations connected to the CMSW and had received an 88 percent overall response. Besides including questions on the new direction of the theology which issued from the Council and on the many aspects of renewal, the survey also included a pre- and post-Vatican belief scale, based on the works of old and new theological formulations.[9] The research team provided over 80 sister consultants to interpret these data. For over ten years, from 1967 to approximately 1978, there followed the special General Chapters to deliberate the agenda of renewal, moving toward constitutional updating.

Conflict Within

By no means, however, was there consensus in all these activities of renewal. On the contrary, there was often deep conflict. The CMSW group lost members in 1971 when a newly formed organization, calling itself *Perfectae Caritatis* and drawing members from concerned CMSW membership, contacted Rome in protest. They objected to the direction the renewal was taking and sought recognition as the true renewal group. Letters from this group were circulated. Among other things, they denounced the survey, warning administrators not to take it seriously and claiming that it had a "this-worldly" social bias. Much of this was done selectively and in secret, excluding officials of the

CMSW. The history of this conflict makes an interesting and humanly passionate story in itself, one which gave rise to some amusing incidents and, in the long run, had a happy ending.[10]

One of these incidents, which I personally witnessed, took place in 1967 when Mother Maria Pacis, IHM, who was on the board of the CMSW, offered to introduce Sister Corita Kent, IHM, at the General Assembly of the CMSW, scheduled to take place the following September. Mother Maria Pacis, known for her adherence to a very traditional style of religious life, had only recently returned from an extended missionary stay in Latin America. Consequently, she was not familiar with the artistic work of Corita and her vibrant seriagraphs which, in one instance, appeared on Boston Gas tanks on the oceanside of the Southeast Expressway, a main route connecting Boston with southern Massachusetts. Sr. Corita had just published *Footnotes and Headlines*, which introduced the religious world to "clown culture" as an expression of the suffering Christ in our times. "Damn everything but the circus"—an e.e. cummings line—danced across posters to introduce this message. When Mother Maria Pacis researched Sr. Corita's credentials, she was amazed at her findings but did not withdraw her offer. Thus, the CMSW had the refreshing experience at the national assembly of seeing two women representing, at that time, a step into the future and a celebration of the past, with the representative of the past making a splendid introduction of a woman with a sensitive and humorous approach to change and celebration.[11]

Because the survey was, in fact, derived from the council documents and directly related to the renewal as mandated, it survived attacks directed against it. The adversarial reaction did, however, delay the usefulness of those findings for some congregations, and temporarily severed their affiliation with the Conference of Major Superiors of Women Religious. In some cases, the data were stored instead of being used. Thus, for some groups, although the renewal process lagged, it was not entirely discarded.[12]

Statements of Mission in the Light of the Council

On the basis of these findings and of many other activities (prompted by the responsible leadership of the CMSW and other regional groups, as well as through the unique initiative of individual congregations), sisters, in a variety of the over 500 different institutes then in the United States, prepared their revised constitutions. These included clearly expressed mission statements, linking the unique charisms of their founders to the unique transition of the church in the world, as expressed in Vatican II and reflected in the survey. Those mission statements are today a central focus of ongoing renewal. Today, almost every institute of women has a mission statement that has developed gradually from membership reflection on their documents, their life and their experience of ministry. Once thought to refer merely to a category of work, the concept of mission today is perceived by sisters to refer to the goal of their work, and the way they do it. Understood as such, teaching, nursing, social service and other responses to human need do not in themselves constitute ministries. Ministry is, rather, the teaching toward the transformation of the world into a just and caring society. It is the providing of health care to all who are ill, not merely and solely to those who can pay. Ministry is the making available to all persons and to all peoples those social services which meet life's crises of age, illness, illiteracy and distress. No one specific ethnic group can now, in justice, be one's sole public. The objective of the elimination of the causal factors of poverty and of related injustices now stands as a primary focus of ministry. Social justice and peace have become the categories for defining the mission; congregational tradition and human ingenuity, the way to carry it out. Apostolic prayer thereby becomes the way religious relate to God; and a community lifestyle, how they relate to the neighbor. The forms of this prayer and communal life are still in experimental stages.[13]

Common to most congregations is a heightened awareness of social sin and the recognition of peoples' rights to self-determination and of individuals' rights to food, clothing and shelter, education and health services, to self-expression and development, as well as to freedom from oppression. These shared values are linked to the salvation theology of a post-Vatican Council church, which calls each congregation to contribute its charisms, in a unique way, to the church's realization of its transforming mission in the world (see *Sollicitudo Rei Socialis*).

This language of the church is familiar now to sisters. Its meaning is constantly reshaping their lives to a new consciousness. To name the goal, however, is not to name what the struggle of the future may be. The direction which it takes responds to the signs of these times. This mission—for justice, for the liberation of the oppressed, for human rights and the development of all peoples—directly links the lives of sisters today to societal transformation. No longer merely one among their many works, this mission is viewed, rather, as a framework for all aspects of their lives and for all that they do. It becomes for them, in all things, a moral imperative and a moral constraint, replacing the external restrictions of religious garb, monastic schedule and cloister.

Some Expressions of the New Perspective on Mission

The unflinching strength of the mission statements that convey a new social justice commitment is exemplified in recent drafts of several of the revised constitutions. These constitutions vary greatly in the styles in which they are written. Unlike their earlier attempts at writing constitutions, most groups of sisters did not begin by consulting canon lawyers on the legal requirements of such documents. After their lived experiences in the 20 years of the post-conciliar period, instead they attempted to incorporate the spirit of their founders and the decisions of their renewal chapters into the documents. These constitutions were designed to be credible to themselves and truly expressive of what they had already begun to do and intended to do in the future. Several congregations of sisters began their revision of constitutions much earlier than did others. They have borne the heat of the day. We will get a clearer understanding of why, if we see what they were saying about themselves.[14]

The School Sisters of St. Francis of the Midwest are one of

those early renewal attempters. They state their objectives in what they call their first principle, which is formulated this way: "We share Christ's mission in the world." Then, after explaining this statement, they specify what it commits them to do:

- to challenge the structures of society to promote justice and human dignity;
- to educate ourselves and others to a greater global awareness and to our responsibilities within the human family;
- to become more aware of cultural diversity in order to appreciate the values and gifts of all peoples;
- to support and encourage Sisters to minister among the poor and oppressed.

The Sisters of Notre Dame de Namur say:

We recognize the call of God in a growing consciousness throughout the world of the dignity and values of each person, race, and nation, and of the ways in which society in its values, structures and systems, denies this dignity (20).

Speaking of the charism of their founder, St. Julie Billiart, they say:

In fidelity to Julie's preference for the poor in the most abandoned places, we choose to stand with poor people as they struggle for adequate means for human life and dignity (17).

Our discernment is rooted in:
the word of God
the teachings of the church
our congregational tradition,
and the voices of the poor (19).

In *The Directives*, a separate section of their constitutions, these sisters define some of the issues they address in carrying out their mission:

> Because of our awareness that unjust structures deny people their dignity, we study the relatedness of global issues. We also join others in an effort to build peace and to search for an end to social evils, particularly war and the preparation for war, world poverty, racism, and discrimination against women. (D3-*Constitutions and Directory* 1984).

The Maryknoll sisters, in revising their statement of mission, defined themselves as "women called to be in solidarity with the poor not as an option but as a sign of the kingdom." The two Maryknoll sisters killed in El Salvador were attempting to realize this mission. In the new constitutions, their statement of mission reads:

> We analyze the religious, social, political, economic and cultural situations in the various countries in which we live and work and discern our appropriate response in ministry in the light of the gospel (9.1).

It continues:

> We commit ourselves to participate in the struggle for social justice, and we respond, both by addressing the roots of injustice and by ministering to those who suffer the effects of poverty and oppression (9.5).

The Catholic Medical Missionaries, the majority of whom are medical doctors, do most of their work in Third World countries. They define their mission in this way:

> Our mission is to those in need of healing, who have few resources, and less power to help themselves: the poor, the sick, the neglected, the unjustly treated, the oppressed. We are aware of the interrelationship of many of the evils in to-

day's world. In the face of global injustice, we, as an international society, involve ourselves in the transformation of the world as we join with others who struggle for freedom, justice, and love.

Their section on the vow of poverty includes this sentence:

By our voluntary choice of poverty, we wish to place ourselves on the side of the poor and in solidarity with them, to witness to the value of fundamental dependence on God and the freedom of spirit this can give.

Note, however, the links of this orientation with their original charism. They have already said that they want to be "an active presence of Christ, the healer," and that "this power compels us to respond to the struggle of the human race and to face and study questions related to life, to suffering, to health and to death in order to bring about that wholeness in which persons attain their God-given potential" (pp. 1, 2).

The Congregation of the Sisters of Loretto is another American foundation that began early to renew and to help others to do the same. In the section of their constitutions on the vow of poverty, they state:

The spirit of the poor proclaimed by the beatitudes demands more than our generosity and detachment. It does demand these. But it also demands a sharing in the struggles of the world against all the evil afflicting our sisters and brothers everywhere. We commit ourselves to work for improving the conditions of those who suffer from ignorance, injustice and indignity. (p. 27)

The Sisters of Charity of the Blessed Virgin Mary say simply:

As women of the church we are called to give strong public witness against oppression brought about by unjust political and social structures—locally, nationally and internationally. (14)

Similarly, the Sisters of the Humility of Mary say:

We find strength in a deep relationship with God and our Sisters as we devote our personal and corporate resources to working toward the transformation of the world...the redemption of the human race and its liberation from every oppressive situation. (p. 1)

In making this statement, these sisters link their documents with the *Justice in the World* Synod document of the bishops of the Catholic church. It is a direct quotation from the 1971 Bishops Synod, that sought to implement the *Call to Action* of Pope Paul VI of the same year, the letter in which he was launching the decision of Vatican II to implement the peace and justice agenda that the council had affirmed in 1965 (Synod).

Although all congregations do not have the same clear perspective on the mission of the church, few have ignored it. Note, by way of contrast, the stated mission of two congregations stemming from the same original foundation: the Immaculate Heart Sisters of Monroe, Michigan, and the Immaculate Heart Sisters of Scranton, Pennsylvania. One is concisely explicit in its articulation of defining how to implement its mission for justice; the other carefully implicit, simply naming general goals:

In our struggle to live the Gospel we recognize our call to serve the needs of God's people not only through the traditional works of mercy but also by working with others to eradicate the causes of injustice and oppression and to help create structures that will promote justice and peace and bring unity among all peoples (p. 8).

The contrast with the following is clear:

Throughout our Congregation's history, we have relied on Divine Providence and responded to the changing needs of the times. We strive to serve in a joyful, loving, hospitable and self-emptying spirit, reflecting that humility and simplicity which present a clear and understandable witness to Christ, who welcomed everyone. In fidelity to that tradition we engage in the apostolic works of education, health care, social service and various pastoral and spiritual ministries. We are also called to incorporate a sensitivity and commitment to social justice in our ministry and to use every opportunity available to affect social structures (p. 2).

Even the physical appearance of most of the new constitutions changed considerably after 1966. Old constitutions were somber and generally unattractive little black books. However, the bindings of most new constitutions now are brightly colored, with artistic symbols on their covers and section dividers. Previously too, constitutions contained few biblical quotations. Today, many of them are rich with relevant biblical references. The old rule books used to be private, available only to those in vows. Now they are shared with those seeking membership. They contain the inspiration for the vowed life and they challenge the members to realize the goals which they articulate. The new constitutions contain the hopes and the dreams of the many sisters who, over the past 20 years, assembled to bring them into existence, and studied, researched, designed and practiced these interim chapter decrees.

The New Challenge

Today, sisters are faced with a new and, for some, unexpected challenge. This challenge comes mainly from those in the hierarchy of the church who fear radical departures from traditional ways. This presents a problem because, in order for the constitutions to be accepted as a way of life in the church, they must be officially approved by the Congregation of Religious Institutes of Consecrated Life (CICL),[15] a Vatican committee that oversees religious congregations to assure their harmony with church life in general. Periodically, over the past 20 years, CICL has issued guidelines for renewal.[16] They have deep concern about the form of governance, a question to be pursued in Chapter 5. They have also set restrictions on changes in the religious habit, prayer life, community, formation programs, and the practice of the vows. Sometimes, some of the modifications suggested are helpful, particularly when groups, in enthusiasm for change, fail to recognize the need of structure, not only for continuity and meaning but for effective action. Other congregations, however, have been asked by CICL to make constitutional revisions which run counter to the responsible decisions of their membership. This becomes a serious problem if the changes contradict both the structures needed for the doing of the mission, as the members understand it, and the lived experience of more than two decades.

Participation in Decision Making

We have seen, in the transition of women religious from nuns to sisters, how religious institutes are called forth in response to the signs of the times. Issues of participation in decision making are of particular delicacy at this time in the history of the church and of its relationship to society. The mission calls for the liberation of the oppressed, a liberation which calls all people to responsible participation in decision making. From the perspective of a given religious group, it is not always immediately clear to those administering the changes what new congregational structures will best realize the values intended, and avoid unintended consequences. For many religious congregations, the decision to develop participation in governance by all the sisters has been implemented in a broad range of success and of difficulty. The learning process for participatory governance and its practice continue, however, as these groups refine their modes of assembly, interaction and decision making, incorporating appropriate modifications of organizational structures, wherever needed. For others, it has focused on the agenda of chapters. For both of these groups, there is no turning back. How this dilemma of obedience to mission and obedience to the decrees of CICL will be resolved involves the meaning of the vowed life itself, as understood by the institutional church historically and as practiced by sisters today. We will explore this meaning in the following chapter by examining the vows of religious life and their practice today.

— 4 —

Vows in the Context of Mission

The vow ceremony is the most solemn occasion in the life of a novice, a member-in-training of a religious congregation. After a preparation of at least two years, sometimes longer, and in the presence of persons representing the congregation and the church, the candidate declares in the terms of a specific formula: "I vow chastity, poverty and obedience." She then must name the congregation within which she takes these vows because the manner of fulfilling them is a specific function of the mission of each group. In the period of renewal, religious congregations looked critically at the forms their vowed life had taken, its emphases and patterns, and at some of the intended and unintended consequences of these. They concluded that, in order to be faithful to their purposes, changes were needed in the way members lived the vows in the present time.

Over the centuries, the original intent of the vows—to give radical Christian witness in an altruistic way of life—had become obscured by the rules set down to make that life operative. The perception, and sometimes even the practice, of the vow of poverty had declined often into an undiscriminating use of goods, legitimated by merely asking one's religious superiors for permission to use them. The vow of chastity had become only the careful preservation of external restraints on sexual expression. These restraints included a combination of cloister, religious garb, and strictly limited contact with the outside world, entered only when one was accompanied by another sister. Finally, religious obedience had come to be interpreted as humble, uncritical submission to the will of an appointed superior, whose commands were received as from God. This distorted institutionalization of the vows gave a negative counter-witness to the values they were supposed to proclaim. The vow of poverty was perceived to allow, in effect, an affluence based on undiscriminating use of resources. The required safeguards of cloister and of religious dress announced both the seeming impossibility for vowed religious to observe chastity without them and the lack of interior discipline implied in their imposition. The pejorative witness of the vow of obedience, as it had become institutionalized, yielded the unfortunate impression of irresponsible submission. Religious unquestioningly acquiesced to commands that were often inadequate to handle many situations—in schools, hospitals, parishes and other church-affiliated organizations. This caricature of the religious life appeared before the public in film and television, in short story and novel. It spawned condescension, amusement, confusion, and even scandal. All this was happening while the people taking vows were striving to live a holy life in response to a call genuinely experienced as from God.[1]

The Purpose of the Vowed Life
The purpose of the vowed life is quite different from that just described. The vows of poverty, chastity, and obedience are the church's creative channels for providing a socially valid structure for a sustained and authentic community life of prayer and human service. What is the individual function of these vows? The vow of poverty implies the choice of a simple lifestyle within which resources are shared with the poor; the vow of chastity, a celibate life controlled by full consciousness of how one's nonpossessive relationships with others can open up to genuine love; and the vow of obedience, a search for God's will and its

realization in ever newer forms, which are linked to the critical social analysis of existing social structures. Discernment with one's congregation, with the intention of responding to the serious demands of the church's mission in the world, constitutes the obedience process for religious today. In the late twentieth century, however, there is not yet consensus on how the goals of observing these three vows are to be realized. Consequently, studies of the vowed life still continue within religious congregations of both women and men.

Most theological commentators on the religious vows agree that the vowed life is intended to be a life of Christian witness. However, the question is: Witness to what? It is true that married life too is a vowed life which gives Christian witness as a sacrament, ever giving birth to a new community and witnessing to the future in its procreative promise. The vows of religion, on the other hand, are intended to witness to a life beyond the present one.

They are directed toward transforming this world in justice, and, in the accomplishment of this end, they are also a radical witness to a life of altruism. They render a relatively few people, living a common life, capable of detaching themselves from wealth and power and, at times, even law, if necessary. The vows express an active free surrender of one's life for others in imitation of Jesus. Sometimes, sisters make this gift of themselves in order to reroute a church on the way to salvation (should the times call for radical change); or, at other times, in order to hold a church steady, when stability is needed. How then is it possible for them to know which are the church's needs in these times?

Reflective meditation on gospel and mission, on individual, community and congregational levels, sparks broad vision, insight and, sometimes, conversion of the committed religious. No less essential are the subsequent observations, lived experience, study and research around local and world conditions—all key elements in the analytic process toward decision making. Also important, but perhaps less rewarding and often discomfiting, is the later stage of the deliberative process, that of acknowledging the unintended consequences of some of the decisions reached, and then deliberating towards necessary changes. American sisters have been and continue to be involved in refining the stringent dynamics of this process of decision for action in a religious and socially valid context.

The Modern Context of the Vowed Life

What then do the times call for today? To answer this question, sisters look to the social teachings of the church to determine direction and to evaluate their practice. The recent pastorals of the American Catholic bishops, developed with grassroots involvement since the Call to Action Conference of 1976 and guided in turn by the hundred years of Vatican social teachings, have become the current source for their review. In their pastoral on the economy, the American Catholic bishops offer some insights in response to this question when they claim:

> We must be a people after God's own heart, bonded by the spirit, sustaining one another in love, setting our hearts on God's kingdom, committing ourselves to solidarity with those who suffer, working for peace and justice, acting as a sign of Christ's love and justice in the world (see *Origins* November 27, 1986).

Commenting on the pastoral in the Boston College alumni journal (Summer 1987), Francis McLaughlin, an economist, points out that: "This language and similar language in other parts of the letter call upon Americans to transform their behavior radically." He is not using the word "radically" lightly. In his article McLaughlin proposes that the letter challenges the assumption that undergirds our economic theory: that we naturally act in our own self-interest. He notes that the bishops' letter suggests that a fundamental improvement in the behavior of men and women, beyond their own self-interest, is a viable possibility. McLaughlin further claims that the pastoral asks for this altruistic improvement in human behavior by showing that to act in self-interest is no longer functional for an effective world economy. He is the first economist I have yet read who is willing to consider an ecomomic theory that moves beyond the classic assumptions of Adam Smith. Smith believed that, since, in his view, humans act primarily in their own self-interest, the economic system must be rooted in the same principles if it is to be effective.[2]

The signs of the times suggest to us today that institutionalizing selfish action is destructive to the development of which the world is now capable. Change, however, toward altruistic living and structures that are altruistic in function and objective, can come only if religion is practiced with sufficient seriousness to create a consistently unselfish moral code of behavior. This means that some organizations—the church, religious communities and other groups—have to demonstrate, living by such rules, that the unselfish love of the other is possible for humans as a way of life. The vowed life in the Catholic church traditionally assumes this possibility.

The Place of Altruism in Modern Society

Why should this altruistic movement toward ensuring the survival of all peoples receive new attention today? Perhaps it is because today the means are more available than ever before. We now have the technological expertise to solve the problems of the world's poor and the resources with which to do it. However, we are not only *not* solving those problems but wasting the resources needed to do so (Neal 1987). In short, we lack the will to devise altruistic systems of production and distribution of resources, and to support essential self-governance among peoples of different ethnic traditions. Some scientists even argue that no such will is possible, given genetic constraints (Wilson, *On Human Nature*). Although Christianity and other religions claim the goal of an all-inclusive and unselfish love, scientists of Wilson's persuasion argue that such love is impossible. Thus, the faith question of altruism is placed explicitly before us today, in contrast with a taught scientific claim to the contrary.[3]

Christianity provides the motivation, the will and the support for radical altruistic experiment. The church, in its new orientation to a mission of social responsibility, is calling its members to realize these new directions. Within the religious community, those in the vowed life direct themselves (by their observance of vows, their lifestyles and ministry choices), primarily to those experiments which challenge encultured poverty, racism, sexism and inherited class advantage. This response is the very reason for their commitment to religious life in the forms which have evolved over the centuries. Often, before the local, regional, national and global communities fully see what needs to be done in the interests of the poor, the oppressed and the disenfranchised, the congregations are already at work, reflecting and experimenting to respond to the gospel imperative in a context of prayer and praise. This is the calling. But can today's religious make the transitions needed to adapt this calling to the challenges and contradictions embedded in modern science and social scientific analyses, and expressed in popular culture? This remains a critical question.

Current Challenges to Altruistic Service

At least two very serious problems face those in religious life today: 1) Not many are responding to the call; 2) the training for religious life, necessarily more professional today in view of the wider range of occupations and activities in which religious now engage, allows the religious other life-options, also viable for service. These can and do draw people away from the vowed commitment. This attrition can happen more certainly if the vows, in the new mission setting, have not been extricated from the outdated formalizations calling for the renewal of religious life in the first place. Probably the most relevant way to pose the questions to be examined is: Is there a need for the vowed life today? If there is a need, what form(s) should it take?

When sisters read the strong words of the bishops' pastoral on the economy cited above, they can agree that the ideals of action set forth in this letter are what they want to realize in their lives. This is why they have been rewriting their constitutions— to respond more effectively to the signs of the times.[4] But they are not alone in doing so. Many in marriage commitments or in the single state echo a similar commitment to this call. They too assent to the church's ever clearer plea to Christians all over the world to change lifestyles and practices from those of conflictive competition between groups to those of cooperative sharing. The church's documents articulate personal or group concerns about racism, sexism and class. Inspired by the ideals of their message, vowed religious collaborate with other caring people in a common dedication to solve the problems of the times. But if this be so, how to respond to some economists and biologists who argue that structuring for this kind of solidarity functions only to the advantage of one's own interest group, since, for them, true altruism is contrary to human nature? But it is precisely this premise which remains an unsubstantiated claim, contradicted not only by evidence from other cultures, but also by the example and life-for-others of countless humanists and religious people.

Structurally, the life of the vows puts love of neighbor before self-interest. Has this priority been more than theory or has it eventually always broken down, at some level of concern for our own survival? I asked a social psychoanalyst to explore that problem in 1967. He did it quite cautiously, basing his conclusions on his own experience and utilizing a neo-Freudian framework. His treatment suggested that the vows can be either a regressive or progressive force. They are regressive if reduced to formalities: cloister to live chastity, permission to use goods to live poverty, and submission to the will of another to live obedience. They are progressive if they embody a commitment to the realization of a social good, for example, of a more just society. He then concluded:

A question today, when most men [*sic*] worship secular idols—the state, the corporation, the powerful—is whether religion will do more than reflect and rationalize the spirit of society. To do more demands a radical reaffirmation of humanist values which might well be expressed in the vows of poverty, chastity and obedience (Maccoby 1967, p. 127).

This conclusion implies that religion may well reflect a social spirit but, if so, that spirit needs basic reform to institutionalize it as the practice of non-self-serving love. Religious congregations and other church groups are engaged in precisely this transforming role today. Christianity challenges traditional Western philosophical assumptions about human nature and its genetic limitations. Earlier in this chapter, I cited two authorities, Francis McLaughlin and Michael Maccoby, the former an economist and the latter a psychologist, because both of them address issues related to the very purpose of the vows in apostolic congregations. The pastoral on the economy and McLaughlin's analysis of it address the major problem of our times: How do we restructure the institutions that produce and distribute goods and services in a global community wherein too many are materially and needlessly deprived?

The psychoanalytic perspective, that of Maccoby, suggests that religion may curtail human freedom in a way that diminishes human development. It is a disturbing possibility. Initially, we may laugh or rail at the picture of religious life popularly portrayed in the media. Then we must indeed ask what it is we are adapting to or seem to adapt to and why? What elements of religious life does the world of entertainment caricature so that people need not take sisters seriously, and what are the effects of such distortion? Humor is a powerful device for preserving the socio-economic status quo with its current division of wealth, power and greed. Possible threats are neutralized, if one does not have to take seriously their purpose, strength and sources. Does keeping vows engender a diminishment of the quality of one's life (i.e., by limiting human freedom and intelligent expression), and yet leave unchallenged institutional structures of power and oppression? I think not. In fact, survey results indicate that only for a minority do the vows become a regressive force of this kind.[5]

However, neither the economists nor psychologists are addressing non-existent problems. It is true that they may sometimes overstate, overgeneralize or, in some other way, weaken the rigor of their disciplines. Nevertheless, significant numbers of people must be acting in their own self-interest, providing evidence for the economist, the psychologist and the socio-biologist to generalize about the naturalness of selfish behavior. Some people in vows must be living them in a diminished way for the economist to see self-interest, the psychologist to find relationships between vowed behavior and dependency, and for the socio-biologist to find in religion only a reinforcement of soft-core altruism (Wilson 1978). Bearing these facts in mind then, let us turn to the question of what constitutes the ideal commitment and living of the vows.

Institutionalization of the Vowed Life

Historically, the vows of poverty, chastity and obedience are called "the evangelical counsels." They are also referred to as the "counsels of perfection" by reference to their gospel sources: Jesus' response to the rich young man that he go and sell all that he had and follow him (Matthew 19:16-22); Jesus' struggle to do the will of his father in preference to his own (Luke 22:42); and Jesus' own celibacy, as well as his advice to some to be as eunuchs while working for the coming of the kingdom (Matthew 19:10).

We have seen, in the first chapter, how the celibate life for women and for men developed slowly to a point of recognition as a holy vocation. We saw also how the solemn vow of poverty became an institution which church authorities resisted changing, lest the inheritance of the land system be upset. It functioned more to stabilize property inheritance for feudal families and to give continuity to a whole feudal system than to exercise an inherently holy influence. In early modern times, this form of the vow of poverty was experienced as repressive for a newly developing urban way of religious life, largely because it prevented apostolic orders to work with the poor of the city. Thus, we can see, from a critical analysis of the history of the vows, that institutions often do develop unintended consequences— consequences which can come to legitimate their continuation in the interests of those who administer them (Merton 1968). This is why periodic review and reform are needed to keep the mission commitment alive.

New Focus of the Vow of Obedience

But what of the vow of obedience? There is evidence that the revised *Code of Canon Law,* promulgated in 1983, has taken into account the new emphases needed for the effective living out of the vows of chastity and poverty. However, it has yet to address the changes needed to make the vow of obedience an instrument of radical risk for the next stage of development in the church, a development incorporating human liberation for a population come of age. The changes needed for this stage have already been set in motion by the Second Vatican Council. The emphasis of the post-Vatican church centers on an option for the materially poor; implementation of this option is an issue of obedience. But an obedience of whom and to whom? For some, it is not always clear. It is this ambiguity that makes the most mission-committed dimensions of renewal of religious life seem like a deviation rather than the good it is, that is, a major growth dimension of religious life in the Catholic church and a valuable contribution to human development in the global community. The lack of clarity which sometimes results in misconceptions about renewal is not necessarily or always deliberate. It is bounded by cultures unable to look to the future, a holding-back strikingly similar to both the reluctance to accept the vow of chastity in the early church; and to change the function of the solemn vows in apostolic congregations in early modern times.

Canonical Definition of the Vows in General

To understand this claim, we look now at how the vows are currently explained and lived by religious, and what changes in their practice have occurred since Vatican II. First, a look at canon law. The Code of Canon Law devotes Book II, titled *The People of God,* Part III, Section I, to "Institutes of Consecrated Life." It carefully distinguishes these institutes from "Societies of Apostolic Life," treated in Section II of the same part and distinguished by the fact that in the "societies," as distinct from "institutes," the members do not take vows, even though they do live in community and do apostolic work.[6] The term "consecrated life" distinguishes those with vows. To what does their consecration through the vows commit all members of all congregations? There are 157 canons devoted to religious institutes. It is from an examination of these that we can see the intent of the vows, as currently interpreted by the institutional church.

First of all, the life is described: "Life consecrated through profession of the evangelical counsels is a stable form of living, in which the faithful follow Christ more closely under the action of the Holy Spirit, and are totally dedicated to God, who is supremely loved" (Canon 573). These are the opening words of the section on religious life. It continues: "By a new and special title they are dedicated to seek the perfection of charity in the service of God's Kingdom, for the honour of God, the building up of the church and the salvation of the World. They are a splendid sign in the church, as they foretell the heavenly glory." Clearly, the new canons portray the vowed religious life as an essential part of the emerging form of the church and of the realization of its mission. Canon 573 relates the vows to the charism of the church:

Christ's faithful freely assume this manner of life in institutes of consecrated life which are canonically established by the competent ecclesiastical authority. By vows or by other sacred bonds, in accordance with the law of their own institutes, they profess the evangelical counsels of chastity, poverty and obedience. Because of the charity to which these counsels lead, they are linked in a special way to the church and its mystery.

The subsequent canon also links the vowed life with the mission of the church:

Some of Christ's faithful are specially called by God to this state, so that they may benefit from a special gift in the life of the church and contribute to its saving mission according to the purpose and spirit of each institute (Canon 574).

Because the vows are contracts made with the church, the

canons indicate that the church controls the interpretation of the vowed life:

> It is the prerogative of the competent authority in the church to interpret the evangelical counsels, to legislate for their practice and, by canonical approval, to constitute the stable forms of living which arise from them (Canon 576).

On the other hand, the canons also protect the obligation of each congregation to preserve its own charism:

> The whole patrimony of an institute must be faithfully preserved by all. This patrimony is comprised of the intentions of the founders, of all that the competent ecclesiastical authority has approved concerning the nature, purpose, spirit and character of the institute, and of its sound traditions (Canon 578).

The Vow of Chastity

Having considered the general purpose of the vowed life, we turn now to the mandates regarding each vow, beginning with the vow of chastity. As we have seen, the vow of chastity is the oldest vow and the one which, in time, came to be protected by the cloister. It was not until the Second Vatican Council that it was deemed possible for a woman to keep this vow without the protection of special identifying costume, particular housing, and strict enclosure. Even today, there are substantial numbers of church personnel who still feel that protective enclosure is essential for women to live the requirements of the vow. What are those requirements? Basically, members of a religious congregation of men or of women agree to forego sexual relations with anyone and to extend a celibate loving relationship to all with whom they live and work. The purpose of the vow is to assure the presence of some loving people to all who need to be loved and cared for. The vow of chastity lived assures people that altruism is alive in the church and that the world is not fundamentally selfish, even though individuals may act selfishly sometimes.

Convent Living

The old restraints of convent living, in effect prior to Vatican II, were neither holier nor more functional to the mission than current lifestyles agreed upon during the renewal period. On the contrary, they created such a psychic distance from others that often sisters were quite unaware of the needs of many human beings, near and far. They were equally dissociated from the interaction that creates communal bonds of understanding and communication among people who work and live together. Because of the restrictions of cloister, sisters knew their pupils, patients and clients segmentally, only in certain aspects of their lives. They were usually quite removed from them in language and perception. Their news, their politics, their work life, celebrations, and home life were realities relatively unknown to them. Despite the artificiality and obvious drawbacks of such separation, some people today would still like that distance re-established. But why? I would venture to suggest: to keep the sisters unaware, so that, as in the past, "the good sisters" might wish to deny or ignore, consciously or subconsciously, unexamined secrets of injustice expressed in regional or local neighborhood behavior. The sisters would thereby affirm, in their unawareness, the legitimacy of certain attitudes and relationships which the vow of chastity was actually intended to raise to consciousness for reflection, action and social transformation. Exploitative race relationships are an example: apartheid is the most striking example of an evil system reinforced in the past by religious beliefs and today challenged by many of those same religions.

In the renewal after Vatican II, in many instances sisters had to relearn how to relate to others in communal fashion and how to discontinue treating others as "externs," as had often been the case in the past. Many sisters and the lay people with whom they dealt had to learn how to relate to one another on a personal level in a way that respected both the sisters' commitment to the three vows and the integrity of the non-vowed. Availability as partners became a question of choice; making wise choices did not come naturally or easily. The canons speak of "the obligation of perfect continence observed in celibacy," and "of an undivided heart." They state that "the evangelical counsel of chastity, embraced for the sake of the Kingdom of heaven, is a sign of the world to come," implying a mystical dimension not immediately understandable (Canon 599). How the vow is to be lived is left to the law of each congregation; but common to all congregations are the limits and directions named here. Clearly, the purpose of the vow of chastity includes sexual restraint as a form of witness and a complete openness to others, especially to the powerless poor and others in need. This mission requires the warmth of genuine love, not the neuroticism of denial and repression. The challenge to religious lies in developing a lifestyle that provides an environment for such love. This is often difficult in a world constantly inviting an exploitative erotic stimulation. But it is possible and, in a highly populated world, the witness of this celibate love is a sign of hope for all—the sick, the abandoned, the neglected, the poor, the unloved, and the perhaps unlovely.

The Vow of Poverty

The vow of poverty mandates a simple lifestyle in order that members be "poor in reality and in spirit." But it also calls for a work ethic: to be "sober and industrious" and to be "strangers to earthly riches." It requires that goods be shared in common and excludes private ownership (Canon 600). The vow of poverty specifies "dependence" in the use of and disposition of goods but leaves the setting of limits to the law to each institute (Canon 600). Since most institutes of women now govern themselves mainly through assemblies, the members devise ways of living and sharing by studying their income, investments (if any), and expenditures, with the aim of carrying out the church's mission to the materially poor always foremost. Thus, there are wide differences in definitions of what constitutes a simple lifestyle. Using shared resources in some kind of common ownership, suggested by early Christianity, is today an obvious solution to some of the problems of world poverty and of local housing needs, to consider just two of many examples.

Because the canons also mandate religious congregations to share their resources with the church and with the needy (Canon 640), new formation programs emphasize that the vow of poverty means now, more than in the past, the sharing of resources with the poor. Practices directed to the implementation of the vow of poverty vary from congregation to congregation, although there are specific canonical parameters for observing the essence of the vow.

There are further considerations relevant to the vow of poverty. The new canons stress that "apostolic action" is "of the very nature of institutes dedicated to apostolic works," that "the whole life of the members is, therefore, to be imbued with an apostolic spirit, and the whole of their apostolic action is to be animated by a religious spirit...and to be performed in communion with the church" (Canon 675). This much closer link of the vowed life with social action points to the need to develop forms of apostolic spirituality, distinct from contemplative spirituality as such but not to be construed as devoid of the contemplative dimensions of prayer. It further demonstrates the church's new understanding of the meaning of its mission to be in solidarity with the materially poor. Institutes are mandated to "hold fast to the mission and works which are proper to their institute" (Canon 677), but to do so within the larger mission of the church in the world. Thus, the vow of poverty now not only invites, but mandates a simple lifestyle, with the purpose of sharing resources in such a way that the dispossessed can repossess the land that is theirs (Neal 1987). This call urges vowed persons into closer contact with the problems of the production and distribution of the world's resources. It strengthens and encourages them to promulgate` necessary changes in favor of those who are in want. The vow of poverty is an announcement of a way to provide for human needs, a way that includes everyone as giver and receiver, a way of Christian witness, however, that is not yet a reality. Living in community is perceived as essential to this new development. The accompanying lifestyles witness to possible solutions for human deprivation, suffered by a majority of the world's population in areas of health, education and other social securities. All these concerns about uses of human resources are aspects of keeping the vow of poverty.

The Vow of Obedience

Faithfulness to the realization of this mission becomes the domain of the vow of obedience, a vow to do the will of God. The challenge is to discern that will in our times. Today, the keeping of this vow is the greatest challenge to members of religious congregations. Redefining the church as the People of God extended its boundaries to encompass the entire globe. (See *Gaudium et Spes*.) It is no longer merely a Roman Catholic church, but a Catholic church, some of whose members hear the word of God and keep it. Many others, however, have no way yet to hear, because for them the church is still embedded in the traditional structures of their oppression. How can this be so?

The study of sociology of religion has made clearer to us that the practice of religion—the prayers, worship, liturgy in song, dance and visual arts—is part of a larger cultural system and hence is bound to the other institutions of a society. The result is that the very practice of religion often reinforces larger societal structures that generate societal norms. This means that the church's regulations, found in law and custom, also come to approve the distribution of power, wealth and prestige in practice in a given society. If the distribution of resources is just, then all is well since the practice of religion will celebrate the society in all its forms. If the distribution of resources is unjust, however, then, unfortunately, the liturgy practiced will still celebrate the unjust society, thus supporting the injustices. At such times, those who suffer from the enforcement of unjust law become estranged and alienated, while those advantaged by it become, at various levels of consciousness, ashamed and guilty, practicing denial in liturgy, song, dance and visual arts. Some even escape into drugs and other means of deadening their awareness of existing and unaddressed evils. Few, if any, remain completely impervious. In such situations, young people begin to resist their culture, many becoming disenchanted by the hypocrisy of the social system, supposedly established for all of the people. At such historical moments, the whole social system becomes tenuous. As Mary Douglas describes so well, it is at these moments in particular that symbols lose their power to control behavior. They die and society sheds them, like a tortoise shedding a hardened carapace (Douglas, p. 179). The evidence of the reality of world poverty, of the rise of Third World peoples, and of the resistance, in centers of affluence and greed, to their struggle to share world resources indicates that *today* is just such a moment.

Current Challenges to the Vow of Obedience

The church's response in Vatican II was prophetic, denouncing established evils and calling us forth to new engagement with political and economic structures. But it takes time to shed the old carapace; it takes vision to create a new system. In the interim, anarchy is a possibility. The fear of anarchy makes the security of fascism (i.e., an unquestioning obedience to the authority of a person representing a center of power) appear attractive to those who fear taking responsibility. Thus, arrogance comes to characterize the structures in which persons do not ask for accountability from those in administrative roles. The risk of periods of transition are very real; life and death are out of balance. Destructive weapons, polluted environments, overcrowded territories, uncontrolled greed, ineffective financial systems, and distrust of collaboration, characterize such moments. Yet these are equally moments of great hope and expectation, especially on the part of the dispossessed. One cannot merely exhort people to continue to follow the rules. The rules no longer work to provide life for the people. There is no turning back.

The transition in our times focuses on human rights.[7] No longer can we tolerate the violent and unjust concepts of a privileged class and subjugated peoples born to serve. One can no longer enforce traditional rules of slavery or serfdom or wage labor without benefits, or military dictatorships. Individuals with too much power, like Hitler, have proved that force can brutally destroy those defined as "enemy" and that the advantaged will not oppose the destruction (Zahn 1969). But, despite such inherent dangers, which society is ready to share power fully and for the common good, to unite in making decisions for which all are held accountable? Who can take on the huge task of reordering societies to the making of wise choices of action in the interests of all peoples? The church itself has assumed this responsibility through the Second Vatican Council. Since this is so, for whom is the related action an obedience?

Fortunately, we are not just beginning this task. Already, concerned people have addressed the issues. Paulo Freire's process of "conscientization," begun in northeast Brazil in the late 1950s, is spreading now to many parts of Latin America and Africa.[8] The creation of Base Christian Communities is a reality in Third World countries. The Medellin conference of the Latin American church approved these new structures in 1968 as a societal transforming method (see Second General Conference of Latin American Bishops, Vol. 2). Freire's method teaches a process of literacy learning which encourages historically dispossessed peoples to reflect, in gospel focus, on the oppressions of their lives. It helps them to raise to consciousness problems of human exploitation, their own as well as that of others, and to take action to change those conditions. At the same time, strengthened by their deep contact with the word of God and with their new bond of hope, in solidarity with their peers, they come to affirm their own personhood and to become aware of their rights as human beings. Literacy is rapidly acquired in this context. In fact, whole communities, illiterate for centuries, have become literate in periods of from six weeks to six months. The method also becomes a process of social development, a stimulus to responsible decision making. However, it simultaneously renders established power groups fearful of what it perceives as the rise of "dangerous masses." The people seem dangerous now, not because they are an undisciplined horde—the fear that the ancient civilizations felt with the migration of tribes. Nor are they dangerous because they are illiterate, ignorant peasants—the fear in the bourgeois revolutionaries of the early nineteenth century. The real fear is that fully conscious fellow human beings, aware for the first time that they have rights that they can reach out to claim in gospel language, will in fact do so.

Freire was exiled from Brazil for spreading this method of rapid literacy learning. Gustavo Gutiérrez has been formally questioned by church authorities for theologizing from these Basic Christian Communities organized by this same method. Church role-players have claimed that the newly responsible local church groups are "too political," even as they recognize their genuine gospel base. Base Christian Communities are but one example of the living church expressing itself through the poor in non-authoritarian settings. The special option for the poor is clearly alive in the church, although not yet in the consciousness of the non-poor. For a hundred years, Vatican teaching has addressed this topic. In many places, it is coming alive now through religious education (Dorr 1983, Evans 1987, Johnson 1986). Liberation theology, rising out of the Latin American experience, is witness to this movement. Skepticism about this theology and resistance to it by some First World church analysts are historical phenomena demonstrating the current struggle between church and state, between manifestations of God's will and the keeping of the law.[9] (See Berryman, *Liberation Theology*, 1987.)

How is this analysis of world conditions linked to the vow of obedience? The canons for the vow of obedience still speak of submission of one's will to that of the superior as the true object of the vow (see Canons 601, 618). After the disclaimers of guilt by obedient Nazis at the Nuremberg trials, religious men and women can no longer honestly idealize a total submission to the will of another human being as a good. We have seen the danger to human integrity in the concepts of loyalty of servant to the liege lord, or of soldier to military officers, demanding a rigid obedience to rule with little or no accountability by the individual for the decisions carried out by the group. A new understanding of responsible obedience characterizes the late twentieth century. It includes the responsiblity of individuals in a community for the communal efforts and actions of their group. Thus, respect for legitimate authority and obedience to agreed-upon norms still hold true. It also includes, however, not only responsibility to participate in making those rules and keeping them, but to understand the effects of their implementation. It also demands reviewing and reforming the undesirable and unforeseen consequences of these decisions when these fall short of the realization of the mission of the church.

Strains on Administrators in Religious Communities

The experience of being in an administrative role has not been easy for women religious in the post-conciliar decades of experimentation. Some administrators, ignoring the gains of this experimentation, still operate in an authoritarian mode, often issuing commands that overstep the limits of their competencies. They are doing so, in many cases, to people who, in view of their own skills and competencies, cannot obey misguided commands. In turn, however, other members may rebel when reasonable and functional commands conflict with their personal desires; or they obey uncritically when the situation calls for a responsible dissent. The ideal of participation by all, in full acceptance of a shared responsiblity for outcome and full accountability for decisions made, is not yet completely a consistent and effective part of group processes. It is, however, now at least an ideal toward which religious obedience aspires. Creative efforts of experimentation, through a variety of governing forms, characterize the plans for government in the revised constitutions of over 80 percent of congregations of religious women in the United States (Neal 1984). It is through the structures of self-government, now seen as one way of implementing the mission of human liberation, that the new obedience is being worked out by women and men in religious congregations.[10]

Another Dilemma

At the request of CICL, an article about obedience to the pope has been inserted into the new constitutions of many religious congregations of women. In one congregation, it takes the following form:

> The Society of the Sacred Heart is an Apostolic Institute of Pontifical Right. With the same love that St. Madeleine So-

phie had for the church and like all religious institutes, we recognize that each one of us, by her vow of obedience, obeys the orders of the pope.

These sisters agreed to insert the recommended article at the very beginning of their new constitutions. This decision was made possible because of their strong tradition of loyalty to the church. Other sisters, however, demurred because specifying obedience to the pope outside the context of their congregation's charism was not in their tradition. They recognized the obedience all Catholics affirm by reason of baptism, but one limited, as for all, to accepting infallible truth. Without intending any disrespect toward or changed allegiance to the pope as head of the Catholic church, many sisters are shocked when they read this article, injected in some form into their constitutions. They know that they neither had nor would have taken the vow of obedience with this standard formulation in mind. They see it, rather, as the commitment of some particular orders, such as the Jesuits, who have vowed a special kind of allegiance to the pope as part of their specific mission in the church. These sisters do not recognize this claim to direct allegiance, separate from the expressed unique charism of their own congregation, as the object of the vow they have taken or will take. Why it has been introduced (or in the case of some congregations, reintroduced by CICL) after having been deleted from an earlier form of the constitutions, is probably a pragmatic decision parallel to the earlier church resistance to chasity as a holy way of life for women and the insistence on the solemn vow of poverty in the apostolic communities of the seventeenth century (see Chapter 1). (More will be developed on this issue in Chapter 5.)

The vowed life today, as all through the centuries, is an integral part of the church in its work of evangelization. An essential component of the church in mission, it is a call to risk all for the realization of a mission bound to a commitment to altruism, the love of the other to which Christians are called to witness by the example of Jesus in his death on the cross. The evidence of today's experience is that the call is not individual in its realization, but communal. No one can respond alone. The Christian call today, as analyzed here, is not one to live an individually holy life in a sin-filled world. In our times, it is a call to join with the dispossessed and the poor to transform the conditions and unjust structures of the world so that all can share more adequately in its abundance and in the stewardship of its resources. Feminism today also speaks to these same ideals, found wanting in society as currently structured. The religious congregations of women, called by both sets of values, find themselves on the cutting edge of the Christian and feminist liberation movements, and moving away from currently institutionalized norms that contradict deeply-held values embodied in the vows of poverty, chastity and obedience. Chapter 5 will address this contradiction in what has become its most salient form for sisters today, namely, in the mission dimension of their structures of government.

— 5 —

Governance
and the Realization of Mission

Many Catholic sisters face a serious dilemma of obedience in the 1980s and will continue to do so in the 1990s. This dilemma takes the form of a conflict between honoring Vatican Council mandates to prophetic ministry and resuming the traditional form of the vow of obedience in the practice of submission to the will of a specific person in a position of authority. In the area of governance, the latest revision of canon law has re-affirmed the sacred character of the decision-making power of one person as administrator and ultimate authority figure—on local, regional and general leadership levels—expressing what is presumed to be God's will for the governed. Set aside and discounted are the nearly quarter century's experiments and lived experience of collegial governance and shared authority, adopted as a model of holiness by many congregations of women religious.

A critical social analysis of the contemporary historical reality reveals that, in order to do this new church mission, new structures need to be established: those specifying a new division of labor and of responsibility, and setting new directions of accountability for those in authority. These functions must give witness to a form of decision making that actively involves all members of an adult community in the planning of its own future. The very words "submission to the will" of another bypass the validity of communal discernment and halt the impetus for corporate direction as expressed in the new constitutions of religious congregations of women.[1]

More respectful of human development and more relevant for achieving desired objectives is the acceptance of a free communal decision to act cooperatively, with the agreement that minority opposition, openly articulated, not destroy the consensus finally reached. Commitment of women religious to the mission of the church has, in fact, led to the adoption of responsible models of participation in decision making. However, approval even to experiment with these new models, already embodied in revised constitutions, is given or held back by a papal commission that has not yet recognized the viability of such cooperative structures. Instead, it still forces governmental models of hierarchy on religious congregations founded to do apostolic ministry in the church. The Congregation for Institutes of Consecrated Life (CICL) has the authority by canon law to accept, reject or refuse modifications in the constitutions of religious congregations of men and women. What are the implications of this intervention for religious?

Since 1965, I have been researching the changing structures of religious congregations of Catholic women in the United States and elsewhere. The findings of my research indicate that Catholic sisters are currently faced with problems that affect directly the third vow, that of obedience. These challenges are similar to those of the early church to the vow of chastity, and in early modern times, to the vow of poverty. Questions posed by my research include:

1. If the mission seems to call for full or delegated participation in decisions that are binding on the membership of a group, but church law calls for a hierarchical structure that gives final decision-making power to one person, which commitment takes precedence and by what means?

2. Can a government, committed to mission, itself come to

perform a prophetic function for the church at one historical moment?

3. Does the institutional church formally deceive itself if it claims that the insights of social science do not apply to church structures in the same way they apply to other organizations because hierarchy has a special charism or grace in the church?

These questions are, of course, faith questions, couched in the language sisters have been using to address the fundamental problems encountered in the past several years of renewal and of rewriting constitutions. The final decade of the twentieth century will be one of a certain urgency for religious congregations. The period of experimentation with new forms of living has ended for many religious institutes and very nearly so for others. Meanwhile, the revised *Code of Canon Law* (1983) has intervened, limiting options for government structures. It is a problem with a history.

Through the centuries in the Catholic tradition, religious institutes of women and of men have been considered "stable environments for living the consecrated life through the members' profession of the evangelical counsels of poverty, chastity and obedience." The belief expressed in the universal law of the Catholic church is that "certain of the faithful are especially called by God to live according to these counsels" and that those who do so "enjoy a special gift in the life of the church and contribute to its mission according to the purpose and spirit of the Institute" (Canon 574, 2). The church governing body has, through canon law, reserved to itself the right to define in broad outline what each of the vows means and how it is to be lived. Definitions of how each vow is to be interpreted are left to the constitutions of each religious congregation and, in turn, these constitutions have to be approved by the Holy See. Some general content, however, applies by law to all congregations: the interpretation of the vows, the relationship to the church of those in public vows (Canon 574); basic points about religious life

(Canon 576); and protection of the autonomy of each institute in developing its style for living the vows according to its own constitutions and particular law (Canons 578, 586, 587).[2]

The canons governing religious congregations are the same for men as for women, except for those men's congregations whose members are clerics, that is, ordained priests. Clerics belong by ordination to the priesthood, which is part of the hierarchy of the church and, therefore, subject to its centralized governance. A non-hierarchical structure is not an option for priests today. My position is that this is a primary reason why canonists did not see the need to examine the viability of the experiments in new forms of governance by congregations of religious women. This code does not yet adequately provide place in the church for some of the alternate forms of governance approved by chapter decisions of the congregations of women. It has not taken into account the fact that these new models have resulted from efforts of the congregations to adapt their special charisms to the mission of the church today.

Governance for Mission

The question of governance in religious congregations is of primary importance both to the congregation itself and to its mission in the world. The description of its structure and practice is a critical component of all congregational organization. Each constitution has to be studied as a unit to determine its viability as a way of life before it is finally given approval by the church through the Congregation for Institutes of Consecrated Life. Although this organization relies primarily on its understanding of the canons in making its decisions to accept or reject revised constitutions, it is still obligated to take into account the special charism and history of each congregation (Canon 587). Therefore, CICL *could* accept a form of government clearly linked to the mission by granting an exception to the still unchanged canonical focus on the vow of obedience to personal authority.[3] This could be done if there were clear evidence in a given congregation that the members were accepting the division and sharing of authority, and concomitant responsibility and accountability.

In other words, the tensions about government in some congregations of women in the church are grounded, to some extent, in the incompleteness of their experiments in participatory decision making. These experiments, therefore, are still formally unassessed for their claimed link to the carrying out of the mission of the church to stand with the poor. A rejection of these new forms of government has serious implications. It implies the rejection or the modification of some of the most dedicated efforts to develop valid structures for religious life in harmony with the mission of the church in the modern world. It also fails to take into account the legitimate aspirations of women to be accepted in fact and in word as equals. As such, they wish to collaborate, to share themselves, their expertise and gifts of mind and spirit in a common effort to service, carried out in a way that respects their own dignity as well as that of others. Such rejection affects the very viability of the life of mission for vowed women today. Given all the chapter time spent in revision of structures, as well as the enthusiasm for proposals for governance approved by chapters, the rejection by CICL risks disenchanting and alienating the most committed of current members and a decline in recruitment of new membership in the near future, even into the next century. The importance of this crisis cannot be minimized.

Were women not choosing to experiment with governance for the sake of the mission, their actions would have fewer ramifications and less significance for the success of their ministries. This, however, is not the case. The sisters have adopted, with enthusiasm, the church's new direction of acting in solidarity with the poor. They have discovered, through their work, that the poor often fail in their efforts to change the conditions of their lives because of their powerlessness in the face of entrenched interests. The predicament of the black population of South Africa is a case in point, as are the efforts of the urban dispossessed to acquire affordable health care and housing in the United States. To work effectively with dispossessed peoples, therefore, some sisters have chosen to learn essential skills of empowerment by incorporating them into their own forms of internal governance.

They thereby learn and practice responsible self-government, which they can then teach to others from the empirical base of their own experience. Through their efforts in so doing, they have discovered their own lack of colleagueship in the church.

Limitations in the Canons

The new canons do not, however, provide much leverage for religious institutes to interpret the vow of obedience in the light of their new understanding of mission. It is indeed true that the vow, as interpreted in the canons, does call religious to follow Christ obedient unto death (Canon 577). This is not the problem. What is a problem is the language and concepts of monarchy embedded in the relationships of obedience at a time when the development of peoples calls for a more peer-like code. Canon 601, for example, delineates a "submission of the will to legitimate Superiors, vice regents of God, who rule according to the particular constitutions."

The canons further refer to one role as "supreme moderator," to be filled by persons who "should rule over their subjects as children of God and, promoting voluntary obedience of their subjects with reverence for the human person, they should listen to them willingly and foster their harmony for the good of the Institute and of the church but always with their authority for deciding and planning for what must be done remaining intact." (Canon 618)

Herein lies the dilemma of the sacralization of personal authority. "Ruling over subjects as children of God" is not a sacred image of responsible decision making. Rather, it is an image which maintains stratified divisions of class and of power, affirming and continuing the dichotomies implicit in such polarities as domination/subjugation and control/acquiescence. These are neither spiritually enriching nor life-giving themes for this socio-historical period. Even though this language similarly applies to institutes of men and women, the effect on women is different from that on men both psychically and practically. This is so because women have experienced a sexist authority wielded over them and their institutes during the long history of the church. For this reason, they are more seriously affected by the use of this language of sovereignty. More specifically, organizations with real power have been consistently controlled by men. In the church, this remains so today. When such archaic language is used now, it inspires, confirms and encourages the old relationships of dependency and unquestioning submission of women to men. Women have learned that these attitudes are destructive of personal dignity and of practical initiative and, hence, ineffective for them and the liberation of oppressed peoples. On the contrary, the concepts embodied in such language are deterrents to the forward dynamism of liberation movements in the late twentieth century. As such, they stand, therefore, in contradiction to the newly affirmed mission of religious congregations of women to do the works of justice and peace in solidarity with the oppressed poor and the dispossessed.

A New Dynamic

This delicate point should be explained. In the context of a book based on the results of scientific research, this analysis is not in itself a manifesto for rebellion on the part of women. It is a description, rather, of the new dynamics which research has yielded. The results reveal that sisters perceive the following as fundamental to their contemporary mission: 1) learning responsible participation based on interdependency rather than dependency; 2) a recognition of new authority, shaped and grounded in trained and apostolically committed competency; 3) a shared use of human skills; and 4) other insights of resourceful collegial governance in behalf of the mission of the church. To achieve these objectives, change must continue or must begin. Developmental change toward reaching such goals is an inevitable and eventual response of faithfulness to the signs of the times. Why these goals?

Among the members of religious congregations of women today are those skilled in analysis of structures of power and decision-making. Committed to the mission, these women cannot accept "in faith" behaviors that they know, in fact, are deficient. They recognize them to be even disastrous, in some cases, for the implementation of mission, especially when uncritical obedience replaces the shared use of trained competency, reflection, planning and corporate decision. Women with professional and technical competencies, who confront the wording of the canons cited, could not in conscience seek membership in religious congregations, unless they were certain that such language and what it implies for affirming a relationship were to change. I believe that such a change is inevitable.

Archaic Language

Many of the new constitutions of religious women call for forms of participatory decision making that define members explicitly as colleagues and peers, who are mandated by vow to divide the labor and to learn the skills for doing it. In so doing, they become mutually responsible and accountable to one another and to the group as a whole. To many, the concept of one person defined as "Supreme Moderator" or even as "Superior" is a contradiction of their growing sense of personal and group responsibility. Sisters have been trying to eliminate the title of "superior" since the beginning of the renewal period. They have substituted titles that more accurately describe the tasks belonging to the roles assigned and accepted. The concept "superior" rose from an earlier setting, when a different understanding of mission prevailed and when the administrator was defined as a loving mother taking care of her children. Sisters cannot afford to think of themselves as children in relationship to one another and then hope to succeed in ministering to people learning to accept themselves and others as peers with shared responsibilities. The label of "superior" is not appropriate for any one person in a community in these changing times. This attitude is not anarchistic. On the contrary, it is related to a greater respect for authority and for the need to use it well. At issue are how authority is shared and accounted for to the members in its use, and how it is understood among adult peers who constitute a community but not a family. In such a community of equals, parental, feudal, and military terms are relinquished, together with their possibly attendant overtones of security and their dependency syndromes. Interdependency is agreed on and practiced, instead, and the charism for mission internalized and implemented.

Uses of Authority

Another real problem which the overly narrow interpretation of personal authority raises for women today, has to do with how this use of authority, invested in one person designated as a superior, has been intentionally linked to faith in God. However, this associative linkage has not been widely successful, and the belief that God acts in a special way through superiors is not held deeply by many sisters today. In the survey of 1980, only 9 percent of the sisters in the United States believed this (Neal 1981).[4] This issue of authority and where it lies might be defined and dismissed as no more than an internal problem in an out-of-fashion church structure, were the issue not so deeply embedded in the mission of the church as a biblical response to the needs of humankind. As sisters learn of these needs, they reflect on Scripture in the light of the signs of the times, as mandated by the Second Vatican Council. They look for the presence of God where the poor organize for survival and a just sharing of the earth's bounty. Sisters worry about the dangers of a totally upward line of authority and command, especially when the leadership of the hierarchy of control is all male and hence limited, inevitably, in its reflections on the experience of oppression and its causes in the current age. The risks of anomie and of alienation are significant.[5]

These reflections leave women in religious institutes pondering the new canons and deliberating the options open to them within the law of the church. They do so because religious institutes of women and men were especially singled out by the decrees of the council to participate in an updating of their entire way of life. Section three of the *Decree on the Renewal of Religious Life* accounts for the extensive revisions in the congregational life of religious institutes which chose to respond to the mandate in the decree. Recall that it says about government:

The mode of government of the institutes should also be

examined according to the same criteria. For this reason, constitutions, directories, books of customs, of prayers, of ceremonies and such like should be properly revised, obsolete prescriptions being suppressed, and should be brought into line with conciliar documents (Flannery, p. 613).

It is also this decree that mandated full participation of the religious congregations in the process of their renewal and "prudent experimentation." The mandate is quite explicit:

Effective renewal and right adaptation cannot be achieved save with the cooperation of all the members of an institute. However, it is for the competent authorities, alone, and especially for general chapters, to establish the norms for appropriate renewal and to legislate for it, as also for prudent experimentation (Flannery, p. 613).

Note that the quotation cited above indicates the "competent authority" to be especially the general chapter. The general chapter is participative and is one of the oldest and most imaginative structures mandated by church law. Its purpose is the shaping of policy and the election of officers in religious congregations. The membership of the chapter is representative of the entire congregation and is elected by the congregation. The chapter elects administrators and provides the particular law for the congregation. It always has both ex-officio members and elected members. Its main function, besides that of electing and policy making, is to review the congregation's quality of life, the effectiveness of the ways of doing ministry, the conditions of the times, and the mission of the church. It also revises its own functioning in response to what it finds to be essential for the good of the congregation and its mission. It is ad hoc, that is, it goes out of existence as a governing body or chapter as soon as its work is completed. However, its decisions remain in effect until the next chapter (Canons 631-633). The chapter usually meets every four or six years. It was through sessions of this body, convoked in all religious congregations, that the revisions of constitutions were effected over the two decades after the Second Vatican Council. For most groups, the period of experimentation and revision came to its mandated closure about 1984. They had complied in obedience to the church mandate to review and renew their life and mission and to revise their constitutions accordingly.

These chapters, mandated to carry out this renewal, began shortly after the close of the council. They allowed religious congregations—ranging from those most open to change to those most closed, due to their previous history and experience—the opportunity to study the documents of the council while they reflected on their own reasons for being. They reflected on their original foundations; they examined their lifestyles, ways of doing mission, prayer and formation of new members. This review was occurring in the late 1960s and early 1970s, when the church, internationally, was addressing most seriously the social justice agenda raised by the voices of Third World peoples (Neal 1977, 1987). This agenda had a marked effect on congregations of women in the Catholic church and especially on the forms of government they adopted.

Structures of Government

One of the striking patterns in the new constitutions of religious congregations of women is that of their proposed structures of government. Most of these are closely linked to choice of ministries and are expressed through a relatively new concept that is part of the ongoing discourse on government. This concept states that government is for mission. It means that the choice of government for religious women becomes for them a form of ministry in itself.

Experiencing within the church what it means to be without power, and, at the same time, living similar powerlessness with the peoples of the Third World, the inner cities and unincorporated rural areas of developed nations, sisters energized themselves by turning deliberation over forms of government into models for ministry. Some sisters, working as missionaries in Latin America and observing the success of Paulo Freire's literacy program of conscientization for liberation, reported their experiences at their chapters. Chapter members, in turn, worked out, from this pedagogical method, similar modes of participatory decision making. They used them not only to administer their congregations, but also to teach themselves how to reflect and act as peers with the poor. In this process, they discovered the competencies of ordinary people, other people like themselves.

Preference for and Perceptions of Forms of Government
Given the limited option of a centralized model of governance, advocated by the new 1983 *Code of Canon Law* for religious congregations of women, to be administered by a "supreme moderator" and her consultant council, it is significant to ask sisters how they perceive governance and its place in their lives. In the 1980 re-test of the Sisters' Survey of 1967, I asked questions relevant to this issue to a random sample of sisters of 20 different religious congregations, selected because they represent a spectrum of positions on pre- and post-Vatican II theology (Neal 1971). Among the 428 items included in the re-test Survey, two were especially relevant to the question of vowed obedience and response to established authority. The responses are indicated here:

1.—Preferred Forms of Decision Making
Item 418: Religious women have experimented extensively with the structure of government in the past twelve years with varying effects. Given your experience and the opportunity to choose, which of the following alternatives would you prefer at this time? (This item was one of 428 items in a national study of sisters in 1980. The response rate was 62% of 6000—3720 sisters.)

1. A government that places decision making ultimately in the hands of lawfully chosen superiors who in turn accept ultimate responsibility for the outcomes and to whom all the members are ultimately accountable.   10%

2. A government that places decision making ultimately in

an assembly of the whole which then delegates authority to administrators who are ultimately accountable to the members in assembly—which assembly is ultimately responsible for the outcomes.   45%

3. A government that places decision making in the hands of lawfully chosen delegates who in turn lawfully choose administrators to whom they delegate responsibility and who are ultimatelly accountable to them.   45%

2.—Perceived Forms of Decision Making

Item 197: Which one of the following methods of administration is characteristic of your community right now? This item was one of 428 items in a national study of sisters in 1980.

1. The major superior should make the decisions with the advice of her council (i.e., central governing group).   9%
2. Council should act as a team making the decisions.   7%
3. There should be consultation with the members of the congregation with the council making the decisions. 22%
4. Committee or delegated group should research issue and report to the council and the council make the decisions.   12%
5. The council should administer decisions made by an assembly and be accountable to that assembly for all policy decisions made.   38%
6. Other   11%

(Totals 99 percent because of rounding off percentages.)

Table 1 details the several responses to an item concerning preferred modes of decision making; Table 2, an understanding of how the present government of each sister's congregation currently operates. The striking consistency between the 10 percent who want a relationship of dependence (Table 1) and the 9 percent who perceive their congregations as operating in this mode (Table 2) indicates that, in many congregations, changes have been introduced in style of government. If we recall that only 9 percent believed that God acts in a special way through their superiors, it would seem that sacralization of their decision making is on the wane. (See note 5.) What is also interesting is that how governance should be done (that is by a single person, a small group, a representative body or an assembly of the whole) is a preference that runs the whole gamut of possibilities. This indicates that the period of experimentation is not yet over and that sisters are still testing their decision-making modes.

Do the revised constitutions in their final form reflect these preferences? Is the Congregation of Institutes of Consecrated Life (CICL) honoring the experimentation in the congregations of women? Are sisters bonded together in solidarity to make their newly developed sense of mission and its relationship to government known and felt by those whose responsibility it is to accept constitutions of congregations of women in the church?

The answers to all of these questions are in process and, as such, still inconclusive. Since the early 1980s, women of recognized leadership have been called upon to publish their points of view as a guide to congregational decision. In the March/April 1981 issue of *Probe*, the newsletter of the National Assembly of Women Religious—(now the National Assembly of Religious Women, to be inclusive of non-vowed women)—called upon Sister Theresa Kane, then president of the Sisters of Mercy, the largest group of Sisters in the United States, to present her position on the question of constitutions and CICL. She opened the debate by suggesting that CICL be recommended to turn over the approval of constitutions to the regional organizations of the International Union of Major Superiors so that they would receive peer review. Her suggestion resulted in a flood of reactions, some of which *Probe* published.[6] They covered a range of differences. Some preferred congregational leaders to engage in constructive interaction, with CICL still doing the assessment. Others gave strong approbation of the proposal made by Sister

Theresa Kane, herself a former president of the Leadership Conference of Women Religious, the U.S. organization of administrators of Catholic congregations of sisters. The National Coalition of American Nuns, a more action-oriented organization in support of minority struggle but considered sometimes too confrontational by some sisters, has proposed an alternative: refusal to submit constitutions and the acceptance of non-canonical status as a reaction to the CICL rejection. This proposal was circulated in mimeographed form in the classic tradition of protest. Interestingly enough, instead of being ignored by official channels of church communication, as would have occurred in the past, it appeared on the back cover page of *Origins*, the National Catholic Documentary Service of the United States Catholic Conference of Bishops, under the headline: *NCAN Expresses Concerns on New Canon Law Code*. The article appeared in the same issue in which the lead article from the Canadian Bishops Commission was entitled: *Alternatives to Present Economic Structures*. This seems to me to reflect at least a glimmer of hope for the possibility of a new tolerance for dialogue in the church, and a realization of the link between organizations of sisters and the institutional structure of the Catholic church as exemplified below.[7]

The Tale of One Congregation

There are many different apostolic congregations of Dominican Sisters. All of them treasure the teaching tradition historically associated with the Dominican Order. Each of them has also its own unique charism arising out of its particular history. All Dominicans value their long democratic tradition which provides full participation of the members through the chapters. At the general level, the chapter is a body that meets once every six years, elects the General Council and sets policy for the whole order, a policy that the newly elected officers carry out and for which they are accountable to the members in the next General Chapter. As stated earlier, the chapter is "ad hoc," that is, its authority ends with the completion of its task, and the next chapter is elected completely independently of the previous one. However, while it is in session, it is the highest authority in the congregation. Decisions it makes must be implemented by the elected officers and can be changed only by decisions of subsequent chapters, except when the decisions made are contrary to Church law and are questioned by the Congregation of Institutes of Consecrated Life (CICL). The latter's exercise of authority is sometimes problematic for members of some institutes today, particularly when imposed in contradiction of chapter decisions on issues that are not clearly defined in church law.

Today, although all orders and congregations of sisters hold chapters in the model described above, there are historical differences. Through the years, some groups had put such emphasis on the personal authority of the major superiors that little was done at a chapter, and the subsequent review became perfunctory. The call of the Second Vatican Council—to use the chapter as the channel for the revision of constitutions and to update them as instruments for implementing council decisions—was the impetus for reviving, or, in some cases, initiating, the authority of the General Chapter.

In the Dominican tradition, however, the recognition of this authority has existed from early medieval times and has continued to the present. As the sisters of one congregation of Dominicans explained to me, in the course of several telephone conversations, once the chapter is in session, the presiding General Moderator becomes just one of the members, with one voice and vote, equal to all the others. The body deliberates for all. After the chapter is over, the General Moderator reassumes personal or ultimate authority, becoming, once again, personally responsible for decisions to be made, but still bound by the decisions of the chapter. In 1980, this group of Dominicans received approval of their constitutions from CICL, but, because Canon Law was in the process of major revision, they were mandated to resubmit the constitutions after the next chapter, which would open in 1986. These Dominicans had chosen a traditional form of governance, which affirmed the personal authority of a General Moderator along with a Council she was bound to consult in certain key decisions. But they also firmly asserted the prior authority of the General Chapter, a decision making body at the local, province and general levels, as part of the long Dominican tradition. To an outsider, this may seem, perhaps, only a minor detail; to a member, there is a world of difference.

In the Dominican traditional understanding of governance, no moderator or any other person of authority can change, modify or reverse a chapter decision outside of the chapter in session. She or he is bound by the belief that the Spirit operates in the General Chapter, assembled to reflect on and direct its life. This is understood to mean acting within the authority set by the institutional church. However, even that authority must be reflected on together in the assembled chapter. That authority, in turn, is bounded in operation by the charism of the Dominican tradition, within which the vows of religion are taken. Whatever decisions or directions a moderator with her council may take are subject to review and reconsideration by the next assembled General Chapter. This norm ultimately preserves or reactivates the tradition and guides the unique mission of the Dominicans in the church.

This is why one order of Dominicans, despite an earnest desire to have their renewed constitutions approved and implemented in the context of their ongoing life in mission, were disappointed when they sent the revised constitutions to CRIS/ CICL in 1987. They had expected that the modifications they had made, based on CRIS's earlier recommendations, would satisfy. They did not. CRIS returned a set of recommendations for further change, in the expectation that the General Council would incorporate them into the document and re-submit it. The General Council explained that they could not do so, since the chapter alone had that authority. CRIS responded in May 1988, honoring this custom but accepting the constitutions only conditionally, that is, until after the General Chapter of 1990, and exhorting that chapter to take the observations made in December 1987 into very serious account. The General Council, in turn, communicated to the membership their own recommendations to be incorporated into the agenda of the chapter. They divided them into two categories: (1) CRIS changes that the General Council supported with a rationale for so doing; and (2) CRIS

changes about which the General Council had serious reserva-
tions. This second category included the reintroduction of customs dropped some 20 years previously, as well as the formulation of the traditional vow of obedience.[8]

Thus, in this instance, the conflict is between two authorities,
that of CRIS (now CICL) and that of the General Council. But
both groups recognize the authority of the General Chapter to
settle the question for the Dominican Sisters.

Another Tale

For many sisters in different groups, it was hard to see the constitutions, so earnestly worked on for so many years, returned
by CRIS asking for modifications and changes (especially in
government structures) which would make the groups more
alike than unique in the realization of their original charisms.
They referred often to the search for God's will, but what constituted that will was hard to confirm. The decade of the eighties
saw significant modifications in the new constitutions. Congregation after congregation capitulated to CRIS. The drafts, coded
for mission in the late 1970s and early 1980s, even lost some of
the spark of justice commitment in the modified forms of their
final submissions. An unambiguous example of this, in the constitutions of one congregation, involved a word change in one
article concerning the formation program that a General Chapter had voted to accept in this form:

> We provide opportunities for a coordinated study of Scrip-
> ture, theology, including a theology of vows consonant
> with our tradition and mission, the history and literature of
> the congregation and social analysis of our contemporary
> reality.

The General Council later allowed a CRIS recommendation to
revise the last line to read: "analysis of our contemporary social
reality." The meaning of the original version, intended by the
chapter, had been to make critical social analysis part of the formal training for membership for all new members. The revision
eliminated that goal by substituting any kind of analysis includ-

ing literary, financial, linguistic or whatever one might choose. In capitulating to CRIS, the governing group had undone a seriously deliberated choice of the previous General Chapter, even though the recommendation incorporated did not redress any canonical violation that could legitimate CRIS's intervention.[9]

CRIS/CICL had some basis for exercising caution in the acceptance of new structures of government. There were and still are weaknesses both in the forms which proposed governments may take and in the way even good forms may be used. This is not the main problem. The problem is how the decisions for the forms selected are made, tested and reformed, and to what end. In the experimental period, as members gathered to deliberate, some groups have, on occasion, experienced anarchy, rebellion, public scandal and real wars of wills. Some newly elected administrators were intimidated by members threatening to resign or to withdraw financial support of the congregation, now more dependent on their often lucrative salaries. The lengthy tradition of unquestioning obedience proved not to have been good training for responsible participation, which, of course, had not been its goal. It did what it was intended to do, that is, free the membership from the tedious decisions that might distract them from their work. But now, that very work—teaching, nursing, direct service to the poor, care of the aged—has the added mission mandate to work directly for the elimination of the problems causing these conditions to persist. Responsible decision-making, accountability to the membership, now fully responsible for outcomes, has become for many sisters a vital part of the gospel-mandated mission for the development of peoples. Hierarchical government in religious congregations, once considered mandated, was voted out, when it was viewed as no longer a witness to the doing of the apostolic works of social justice leading to world peace. Works of charity could still be done effectively in the old model, but not works of justice. The new worldwide understanding of the human rights of all peoples clarified the need of systematic education and training of peoples so that they might seek their share responsibly as partners, and no longer as objects of pity or scorn (see *United Nations Bill of Human Rights* and *Pacem in Terris*).

Sisters were now faced with the dilemma of choosing between obedience to a personal authority or obedience to the realization of a mission. Conflict has developed within some congregations. The membership has divided. One group of Sisters of Notre Dame became a test case. With full knowledge of the experience of other congregations whose constitutions were sent back by CICL for revision, but feeling, in deep faith, that their model of participatory governance reflected their historical mission "to go to the poor in the most neglected places," they voted, in the General Chapter of 1984, to continue their 20 year experiment with fuller participation of members than the CICL review of constitutions had thus far allowed.

To allow for cultural differences, the chapter mandated each province or unit to construct its own form of government at the intermediate level and to do so in assemblies called for that purpose. This was done to honor differences historically related to their many locations in Britain, Belgium, Italy, the United States, Zaire, Japan, South Africa, Zimbabwe, Brazil, Nigeria, Kenya, Peru, Nicaragua and, later, the Sudan. Each unit would study, experiment with and develop its own model. Local residence groups would be collegial or centralized by choice. But whatever form they chose, they would then be responsible to live within the strictures of that intermediate form. This was not an easy transition. It was especially difficult for the U.S. provinces, of which there were six, because of highly trained professionals, many of them very strong-willed women as they addressed the experiences of their local missions and communities. It is not easy to take on responsibility for playing by the rules when the rules are new and the outcomes less predictable.

Another test case in 1988 became a "cause celebre," as two sisters, both deeply commited to the local mission in a center for poor women in West Virginia, took a strong position on a woman's right to choose in the abortion controversy. Catholics for a Free Choice took up the cause of Barbara Ferraro and Patricia Hussey, both members of this congregation of Sisters of Notre Dame. The central governing group, residing in Rome and constituted by two British sisters, one Belgian, and two from the United States, was hard pressed to deal with the insistent demands of the United States television media and the press. Even though they felt quite certain that the sisters were making a responsible choice in their own conscience position on abortion, they decried the fact that their public image had evolved into seeming "pro abortion."

The Boston and Connecticut province administrators, as the responsible intermediators, tried to keep the channels of communication open. The Boston province sisters met in open assembly and expressed strong, even passionate opinions on what actions to take on the issue. They finally agreed to support their sisters in West Virginia, even though many did not affirm their public stance nor their public criticism of the decision-making process. It was a hard struggle, with a significant social justice component, at a time when the church was torn by division regarding the role of individual conscience in the question of responsible choice. The Boston sisters developed a strong solidarity, as they met each other's diverse understanding of and positions on the issues. It was difficult for all who had to make the choices. Many were saddened when Barbara and Pat chose to sever their membership; others were relieved. All felt they had entered a new era of responsible participation. The eighteen–year–old Boston province felt that it had passed the first big test of taking command of its life in mission. They did not see a clear road ahead but there was life and hope.

The dynamic of this incident, four years in process, was a major factor in determining a decision made by the General Governing Group, itself structured as a team accountable to the membership by the constitutions voted in by the Chapter of 1984 but not, at that time, accepted by CRIS. The decision was to revise the structures of government in the Constitutions of 1984 to conform to the recommendations of CRIS/CICL, some but not all of which were canonical in content. They sent their revised version to the provinces, asking whether or not there was a preference to submit that new draft to CRIS immediately or to wait until the next General Chapter.

Some sisters tried to explain that revisions of constitutions developed by any group and not subject to prior General Chapter review were not valid, even if the group that made them was the General Governing Group itself. Others affirmed the right of the Governing Group to make changes for the members. There was no consensus. Close to 500 sisters, about one-fourth of the members, wrote personal objections. Some provinces called meetings for serious discussion; others felt the mandate to do this was not existent. Each was acting according to the intermediary system they had initiated. All were experiencing the dilemma posed in the Dominican case but without the strong backing of a very long Dominican tradition. Whose authority within the congregation is final with respect to constitutions, that of the chapter, where they are shaped and changed, or that of the governing group, when so ordered by CRIS? Late in December 1988, the governing group decided to submit to CRIS/CICL their revision of the constitutions for approval, which came immediately. The constitutions are currently (1989) being distributed to the entire congregation. What is gained and what is lost?

The Sanctity of Personal Authority

The thesis of the sanctity of submission of will to the personal authority of a single major superior is currently an on-going problem for many orders and congregations. The rationale for its holiness was carefully and analytically presented by Sister Mary Linscott, SND, in the March/April 1983 issue of the *Review for Religious,* one of the two most commonly read journals about consecrated life in the United States today. According to her point of view, there is a holiness, a sacred quality or what she calls a "religious" quality in submission of mind and will to a command made by a particular person in elected office in a religious congregation, namely, the "supreme moderator."[10]

The concept of government for mission is questioned by such a premise. If the recommended form of government for mission calls for a fuller participation in the actual decision making by the members, it spreads the charism of decision, beyond the ultimate responsibility of one person, to a search for the expression of God's will by the whole congregation in mission. Recognition of the variety of experiences of the members of a congregation, their shared commitment to community and mission, as well as reflection on the uses of authority through centuries, all suggest that there is a more effective way to act today than by relying on the charism of one person's authority.

Government as a Form of Witness for Mission

If government is for mission, then every obedience is discerned in the context of membership. Authority, that is, the right to use power, rests in the members who, by reason of this responsibility, must discern what is the will of God, the authentic object of vowed obedience. This linking of governance and mission poses a dilemma for those experienced in governance. Moving from the old direction is, in effect, the rejection of dependency, and living with the new seems open to possible selfishness, a consequence which the new goal seeks to avoid. The new objective is that of responsible and informed decision making, in which the community holds itself accountable for the outcomes of its choices. Skills in communication and deliberation are not yet consistently and universally well developed. Like the rest of the modern world, sisters may sometimes manipulate symbols. Sometimes intentionally and sometimes unwittingly, self-serving interests may cloud the doing of the mission. Therefore, until they can responsibly implement the structures they have put in place as the primary guide to action and decision—the very reason for their being vowed religious in the first place—sisters must walk where there is no path but where, one hopes, one walks with God.

What is to be done on a practical level remains an open question. This study is not a handbook. It expresses principles, information and research results, the latter in a form not yet conclusive, but presented here because it seems, at least to this researcher, that it represents an important movement in a time in which religion is playing a critical role, both on the right and on the left. We who are practitioners within this context are just as responsible as everyone else to disassociate the practice of religion from the exploitation of peoples, and to associate it with the charism and gospel of the church.

Faith and Organization

I close this chapter with a brief discussion of a theological item from the 1980 Sisters' Survey re-test. It places my research in the context of our times. It is a selection from the chapter decrees of one of the congregations in the study. It reads:

> Inherent in our developing understanding of mission is the belief that God, who continues to speak to us in diverse ways, today calls to us with special insistence through the voices of the dispossessed and the materially poor as they attempt to organize themselves to claim their rights as human beings. (Item 395, re-test Survey, 1980)

Seventy-nine percent of the sisters agreed that this thought was reflected in their revised constitutions; 77 percent believed that it was true of their experience.

If this statement is theologically sound in the Christian tradition, and I think that it is, it would seem to me that the efforts sisters are making to find effective methods of participation in decision making are well worth the struggle to continue. Several centuries of theological reflection have informed their understanding of who God is. Currently, however, judging from the changes they are introducing, the more pressing question for them is not who God is, but *where* God is. Rather than resting with the easy assertion that God is everywhere, they are seeking God where the poor gather in city, town, and rural areas claiming their human rights. Some sisters are joining the poor in that action. They see as an immediate goal the development of sound decision-making structures for full participation of the poor as peers in the effort to eliminate human misery and to liberate peoples. Other sisters, working with the non-poor, are seeking to elicit altruistic responses to the just demands of the poor as they reach out for what they need to survive. This interactive vision is biblically sound and it fits the signs of the times. Its implementation is an agenda in process. It constitutes a challenge, a promise, but not yet a fully realized program of action. The sisters involved in this agenda do not perceive themselves as working alone, but rather as part of a world movement toward a justice and peace program that is beginning to emerge in many different religious and other contexts that are a vital part of human life today.

Epilogue

The tortoise has been walking through the pages of this book. It has moved slowly, its hardened shell casting an ominously rigid shadow whose contours seemed at times forever fixed. But we have seen the tortoise emerge at length, deliberately vulnerable, risking its safety to foster new growth and new life. The image of the tortoise has served here as an apt symbol of the centuries-long development of religious congregations of Catholic sisters. The composite carapace of an outmoded institutional framework and accumulated customs finally shed, these congregations now allow their members an environment for a more faithful response to their apostolic ministry in the church.

We have seen how their response to Pope John XXIII's call to *aggiornamento* and to the Second Vatican Council's *Decree on Renewal of Religious Life* set in motion over 20 years of study, prayer, and experimentation, succeeded by reflective evaluation done in a biblical context, an old custom initially revived in the Sister Formation Movement. As a consequence of the long preparation and practice, an accelerating enthusiasm for the social justice agenda of the post-Vatican II church has marked the renewal of most congregations of women in the United States. The subsequent refinement of mission, derived from the social teachings of the church and examined and tested during the renewal chapters, has taken place at varying paces and degrees of intensity. This careful process has set the directions for the next few decades toward developing a central criterion for mission and choice of ministry an appropriate response to the just demands of the poor.

Shedding the Carapace

The old carapace of uniformity of appearance and order of life has been left, reluctantly by some, in the old monastic settings. For some sisters, there is still deep nostalgia for elements of that former life of silence and contemplation which took precedence over any action of service. In fact, the prayer, the contemplation and the quiet reflection remain, but they are focused on an active mission that cannot wait. Once human awareness is raised to grave problems of neglect, rule of life must give way to social action. So it is that, in their many congregational chapters, sisters, inspired by the particular charisms of their founders, continue to put in place those lifestyles adapted to their new understandings of a call to mission.

Many of these sisters are ex-nuns, who, although occasionally nostalgic for the other-worldly orientation of the past, yet, stimulated by the council, welcome the transition to the present. Still others never knew that older style. Their minds and hearts are attuned to the post-Vatican church and its struggle to find effective new ways to bring Christ's message to the world. The more intense demands of work and community service require change in the rules of daily life. Sisters' experimentation with patterns of prayer, meditation, liturgy, communal living and the order of the day focuses now on the mission of social justice as a pressing moral imperative. As the Sisters of Charity foresaw in the seventeenth century, congregations now perceive the need of their members' presence on the street rather than in the convents, in the local churches rather than in the private chapels. The sisters are praying today with the people at parish liturgies. They are challenging the very quality and purpose of those liturgies, particularly if some of God's people are excluded from the community of worship, or if the service ignores the fact that

God is with the poor as they struggle to claim their human rights.

Youth and Mission

Membership in religious congregations of Catholic women is growing in African and Asian societies. Something quite different began happening in the old European countries around mid-century, that is, a long and steady decline in new members. In the United States, this decline begins later, actually taking a precipitous shape only well after the Second Vatican Council. Despite the decline, however, young women of deep integrity are still choosing to join these groups. They have been moved by reading their mission statements, as expressed in the revised constitutions, and by reflecting on the promise they hold for transformative action in society. They are inspired by the justice and peace agenda ever growing in the church. These newer members are much older when they arrive than were their counterparts of the 1950s. Their average age is 26. All of them have work experience; most of them, a college degree and often an advanced degree as well. They have had the experience of owning their own car, living independently in an apartment, taking care of themselves in the recreational give and take of young adult society. As members, they expect and accept much more participative influence in the congregation than did their forerunners. Working in committees, they help shape the formation program; attend chapter planning groups, make judgments about the quality of participation; and join school, community development, and service programs to effect change in situations characterized by racism, class and sex discrimination, but most especially by poverty and deprivation. They know that strong community bonds are essential for effective action. They want to learn how to pray, to meditate and to live as sisters. They like to be known as sisters. They are the sisters of the future. They call all of us to action for justice. They are faith-filled people, eager to know about the founders. They listen to stories of the very old. They want an experience of "the mission." They deeply believe in the vows. They are not seeking a third way. They are impatient with pettiness, professional jealousy, worldliness. Yet, they are very much of this world. They come from old ethnic groups, newer Hispanic groups and some are African-Americans. This mix is new. Where these new members will be going is not clear yet but they will make the path.

The Call to Congregational Religious Life

God's call is still there. So is the response of the sisters. Yet their lifestyle is in flux. For the most part, sisters live in small communities of their own members, though some live now in mixed groups of members of different congregations, or with lay associates, or in other settings. Praying together daily, preparing meals for one another, sharing household tasks, and, on occasion, celebrating liturgies (usually with a wider community than the residence group), going out daily to several different kinds of ministries, attending many planning meetings, giving and receiving counsel and, at times of retreat, going apart to rest awhile—these constitute the life patterns, some quite new, for today's women religious. There are worries about the cost of living, care of the elderly sisters, and where the new vocations will come from or even if they will come at all. Many congregations have not had new members for over ten years. Others, however, although they have fewer new members, are sought out by those who have the same enthusiasm for mission and sense of calling that have characterized sisters down through the ages. Furthermore, for some groups in Third World countries, the number of new members is rapidly increasing.

Although the faith commitment is deep, still God's presence is not easily celebrated together because each community of sisters is exposed to a wide range of church liturgy and sacrament, some of it life-giving and sensitive to the demands of the poor, others insensitive to the reality that there is a new direction of service called for by the Second Vatican Council. Some local church liturgies are celebrated with an unawareness of the social justice direction of renewal and still others, as has been true historically, are explicitly resistant to the justice agenda. Sisters today are far more aware of the problem of a co-opted church than they were prior to the renewal because they are, through their formation, not only more informed on social realities but more skilled in analyzing the interaction between the church and the society in which it is situated. Their responsibility is, therefore, much deeper for addressing questions of social justice. This new burden of responsibility is mainly what led to the lifting of the hardened carapace, which, in the past, protected their transcendentally-oriented life, but which now blocks the church's transforming mission in a society needing witness and action for justice.

In fact, the co-optation of local churches to established interests, much more apparent now to sisters trained in critical social analysis, has become a scandal to some, an anguish to others and a source of deep indignation to those whose very works of service find their strongest resistance from men and women in traditional church roles. These are painful realities that sometimes seriously disenchant those who are committed to mission and who try to be faithful to expressions of faith. The limited role allowed to women in the church is a source of alienation, not only regarding participation in worship or response to a call to ordination experienced by a small but significant few, but also in the effect of this limitation on participation in critical decision making within the church, where especially the groups making the decisions are limited to men in ordained ministry.

These problems and pains do not have the same patterns in all settings. In many Third World settings, where the poor struggle for survival, worship and action for social justice changes are often closely linked in the same struggle. Often too, however, in another part of the same town, a church indifferent to the struggle provides a conserving worship for the more affluent faithful.

Going apart to rest awhile, to pray, to meditate, to strengthen the will to persevere is still as much a part of religious life as it always has been, and the intensity of prayer is often greater now. Many more lay men and women now join religious congregation members in common efforts to prepare for church mission and to carry it out together. Some priests also share the same vision. The vision of a just society is an ever growing awareness of God's presence where the people lift up their burdens and joyously enter the city. A sense of challenge resides in the apostolic religious calling and the problems to be solved keep alive the hope of new forms to come. But, at the moment, the tortoise has shed the old outer layer and the design of the new carapace is not yet clearly delineated. The sisters are walking where there is no clear path. They continue to walk, in the light of the Gospel, to where God is—not only to where the cries of the poor, the suffering and the helpless call them and to where those who cannot cry out are, but also to where the newly aware and organized poor reach out to take their place in shaping the future of the just society.

Notes

Chapter 1

1. The concept of implementing the council's call to action is found in section 48 of Pope Paul VI's encyclical *On the Development of Peoples*, 1967. The Medellin Conference of the Bishops of Latin America, in 1968, was the first continental response to that call. This event marked a transition in the Latin American church to a substantial identification with grassroots groups called Base Christian Communities. The corresponding event in the United States was the Call to Action Conference of 1976, Detroit, in preparation from 1971 onward. This was the first time that local churches in the United States met nationally. The more than one hundred proposals from this conference, voted into policy by the Bishops in May 1977, were the basis of the Sisters' Survey of 1980. The discussion of mission in this chapter focuses on this survey: see *Origins*, Vols. 6, Nos. 20, 21, 48; Vol. 7, No. 44; vol. 11, No. 10; Neal 1981.

   The earliest regional Catholic initiative in the United States to implement the synod document on justice was the pastoral letter of the Catholic Bishops of Appalachia in 1974, *This Land Is Home to Me*. The most recent documents are the national peace pastoral, *The Challenge of Peace: God's Promise and Our Response* (*Origins*, Vol. 12; No. 20, 1983); the Bishops' pastoral on the economy, *Economic Justice for All: Catholic Social Teaching and the U.S. Economy* (*Origins*, Vol.16, No. 24), November 26, 1986; and on women, *Partners in the Mystery of Redemption* (first draft, National Conference of Catholic Bishops, March 23, 1988).

2. This formulation is from the Chapter Acts of the Sisters of Notre Dame de Namur, Rome, 1978, p. 12. It was incorporated as Item 395 in the Sisters' Survey of 1980. See note 8, below.

3. Since the Uppsala Conference of the World Council of Churches in 1968 and the Medellin Conference of Catholic Bishops in Colombia in the same year, several ecumenical organizations supporting Third World initiatives have come into existence. The Washington Office on Latin America, the Washington Office on Africa, and the Coalition for a New Foreign and Military Policy, and the African Peace and Justice Network are examples. Each of these groups represents several church organizations.

4. Jo Ann McNamara's *A New Song* is a careful examination of original documents of these three early church writers. She is preparing an additional historical work which will bring her history of nuns and sisters up to the present.

5. The rule of St. Benedict dates back to the sixth century. For an interesting account of its development in religious orders of women, see *True Daughters: Monastic Identity and American Benedictine History*, by Judith Sutera, OSB, Mount Saint Scholastica, Atchison, Kansas, 1987.

6. Most of the sources I am using for this section will be listed in the reference list under "Sister" because, although the accounts of founders and histories of religious congregations of Catholic women are usually full-length, carefully documented published books, they often are authored anonymously by a sister of the congregation or in conjunction with a priest author, whose name alone appears on the title page.

7. The study of archives of religious congregations is a rich resource of historical and social records barely touched to date. Notre Dame University has established an archive at the Cushwa Center for the Study of American Catholicism. Materials on the history of nuns and sisters can be found there. In the 1980s, renewed interest in the archives of religious congregations of women has developed with the realization of how little is known of their pioneering work. The Conference on the History of Women Religious, for example, sponsored by the Cushwa Center at Notre Dame University and funded by the Lilly Foundation, now meets periodically and publishes a newsletter. It brings together some 200 archivists and historians.

8. From 1950 through 1965, many books on the updating of religious congregations of women were published in France, England and the United States. The editors were frequently priests in religious congregations who provided pastoral direction to the major superiors and to the formation directors of congregations of women. On the vows of obedience, they had a distinctly authoritarian point of view; on educational development and elimination of quaint customs, they were stronger in the United States than in Europe; on mission, they presented a secondary emphasis yet did indicate a growing awareness of the new priority of the justice agenda. See Haley, Ple, Sister Rita Mary, Sister Florence. For an extensive listing of this literature, see Kolmer 1984.

9. The major organization working for a combination of professional training and a sound theological grounding was the Sister Formation Conference, founded in 1953 by a group of Sisters in the National Catholic Education Conference. They surveyed religious congregations to determine

the actual extent of formal education in religious congregations of women as part of planning to upgrade education programs where needed. They solicited the cooperation of Catholic colleges and universities in the project. This group was sponsored jointly by the National Catholic Education Association and the Conference of Major Superiors of Women, later renamed The Leadership Conference of Women Religious (LCWR). This project had the full cooperation of the Congregation for Religious at the Vatican. See Sister Rita Mary Bradley, Ed., *The Mind of the Church in the Formation of Sisters.*

10. In 1965, at the invitation and under the sponsorship of the Conference of Major Superiors of Women Religious, I began a series of surveys. These included: a detailed administrative report of the general resources and plans of the congregations in 1966 based on information received from administrators of 437 religious congregations or provinces; a population survey, in 1967, in which 139,691 sisters responded to 649 questions; a content analysis of the special general chapters of 280 different congregations in 1974; in 1980, a random sample re-test of the opinion survey, sent to 6000 sisters in twenty congregations selected on the basis of their belief scores in the 1967 Sisters Survey; and a second detailed administrative report, updating that of 1966 and indicating trends for a thirty year period, responded to by 342 groups in 1983. The analyses of these data constitute a longitudinal study of the transitions initiated by the *Decree on Renewal of Religious Life,* issued by the Second Vatican Council. The material for this section is based on those data. Reports of the 1966 study are in the *Proceedings* of the CMSW for 1967 and 1968. Preliminary analyses of the 1967 survey are in Neal 1970, 1971, and in a *Sister Formation Bulletin* of 1969. Neal 1981 is a preliminary report of the 1980 survey. The congregational report, which compares the 1966 with the 1982 data, is published as *Catholic Sisters in Transition From the 1960s to the 1980s,* Neal, Michael Glazier, Inc., 1984. For the background rationale for this study, see Sister Mary Ellen Muckenhirn, *The Changing Sister,* 1965. Formal systematic analysis of these several data sets is still in process.

11. Current research is testing this hypothesis. It will be reported in the final monograph on the Sisters' Survey.

12. See, particularly, Pope John Paul II's 1988 encyclical, *Sollicitudo Rei Socialis.*

13. These themes are most commonly expressed in liberation theology coming mainly from Latin America. See Gutiérrez, Miguez-Bonino, Tamez, Sobrino, and Richard. See also *The Just Demands of the Poor,* Neal 1987. In 1989, Orbis Books published a volume expanding the consider-

ation of liberation theology to other areas of the world called *The Future of Liberation Theology*, edited by Otto Maduro and Marc Ellis.

14. See "Report to the Vatican/U.S. Religious Orders Today," in *Origins*, April 20, 1978, Vol. 7, No. 44, pp. 691-693. See also: "Church Leaders Confer on New Role of Missions," *New York Times*, May 10, 1982, p. B6; and "Guidelines for the Study and Teaching of the Church's Social Doctrine in the Formation of Priests," *Origins*, August 3, 1989, Vol. 19: No. 11, pp. 169–192.

15. *Codex Iuris Canonici*, promulgated early in 1983, provides for a strong mission commitment in the treatment of the vows of poverty and chastity, but not for obedience. There is evidence in the formulations that a serious area of tension for future congregations of religious women will be that of trying to keep the vow of obedience faithful to the canons and at the same time to be obedient to the mission of the Church. I predict that, in the next revision, these two foci will be combined into one, but that the new focus will be related to significant change in church structures of decision making.

Chapter 2

1. Both Alexander Haig, then Secretary of State, and Jeanne Kirkpatrick, the U.S. representative to the United Nations, within twenty-four hours of this occurrence, made remarks on televised news broadcasts suggesting that these women were gun-runners or, at least, Communist sympathizers.

2. It is not possible in this short essay to present the full impact of the local churches of the Third World on the renewal of the life of apostolic women. Much has been and is being written on the Base Christian Communities. Several doctoral dissertations are in process and some already published. See Berryman, Adriance. See also Jeanne Gallo, SND, *Basic Ecclesial Communities: A New Form of Christian Organizational Response to the World Today,*1988.

3. The accounts of the reflective action for social change characteristic of the Base Christian Communities of Latin America are now a part of the active history of the church in the Third World. See, especially, Berryman; Adriance and Gallo (in bibliography). On the rights of the poor to take what is rightfully theirs, see *The Pastoral Constitution of the Church in the Modern World*, #69.

4. See the South African Bishops' "A Stand Against Apartheid," reprinted in *Origins*, March 23, 1977 (Vol. 6), and *The Kairos Document*, circulated in

1985, in which 101 South African theologians and other church people distinguished three different theologies addressing the apartheid condition.

5. United Nations' documents reinforce church efforts toward the development of peoples. (See John XXIII's *Pacem in Terris*, 1963; Paul VI's *Development of Peoples*, 1967; Call to Action, 1971; the Bishops' Synodal document, *Justice in the World*, 1971; and John Paul II's *On Human Work*, 1981). The United Nations has produced and voted into existence a covenant on human rights—*The International Bill of Human Rights*, United Nations, 1978. In it, for the first time in history, "the rights of all peoples to self-determination and to enjoy and utilize fully and freely their natural wealth and resources" is fully recognized as a basic human right (UN, 1978, p. 2). This recognition encourages Christians to join forces with Third World countries to help them to achieve their rights. But this new stance also creates problems of danger and of risk. The new order calls on the old church to change its former allegiance, to resist its own prophetic message no longer, and to break away from the agents of destruction whose ally it had become. In the process, sometimes the prophets of change are killed. The powerless are most threatened. But now the dispossessed are not alone. Among many church initiatives over the past twenty-five years, religious congregations of Catholic women have become a vital part of this new orientation to human rights and development. They have joined the world's peoples struggling against poverty. They have done so especially in the fields of education and health care, as well as in the way they provide other human services.

6. When the Pontifical Commission on Religious Life, comprised of Archbishop Thomas C. Kelly, O.P., Bishop Raymond Lessard and Archbishop John R. Quinn, was mandated in 1986 to explore the reasons for the decline in religious vocations in the United States, they set up a committee of religious which was commissioned to provide data on the ongoing life of men and women in congregations and orders since Vatican II. Since the data on the women were already gathered in *Catholic Sisters in Transition From the 1960s to the 1980s* (Neal, 1984), it was used to provide the needed research. The Center for Applied Research in the Apostolate was commissioned to provide comparable data for the men's groups. See *New Catholic World*, January/February 1988. See also Hose and Verdieck in the Bibliography.

Chapter 3

1. There are a variety of forms of religious life treated in canon law. The word "institute" includes all of them. Most of these organizations, founded before the Council of Trent in the sixteenth century, are called

orders. Those whose members do apostolic works are usually called congregations; they are called secular institutes if their members do not live in community. Those whose members take no public vows are termed pious societies. There are also individuals who live with private vows. They are called "hermits" and/or "virgins." See the new *Code of Canon Law* for these distinctions. The groups I am writing about are, in the majority, congregations, though a few are orders. For general reference, I will call all of them congregations.

2. This term today raises objections from a newly dedicated laity, who, in the course of their own renewal, consider their affiliation with the church equally religious. There is no intent, in its use here, however, to stratify or to separate, but merely to designate the members of religious congregations referred to in this study. The Pastoral Constitution on the Church in the Modern World, *Gaudium et Spes*, the most fundamental document of the Second Vatican Council, recognizes all the members of the church, actual and potential, as "the People of God." It also defines the historical distinctions that are clearly stratified and which include a division of labor: the hierarchy, who service the community through teaching and maintaining good order, that is, by governing and sanctifying; the laity, who seek the kingdom of God by engaging in temporal affairs, ordering them according to God's plan; and the religious, who live the evangelical counsels, communally sharing what they have, who they are and how they make decisions. This traditional division of functions is frequently challenged today by groups of men and women in the church (for example, Women Church, Quixote Center, and National Association of Religious Women). The first of these, Women Church, develop women-centered liturgies and prayer forms; Quixote Center is made up mainly of priests who affirm the ordination of women; the third, NARW, works to eliminate the distinctions of privilege between women in the vowed religious life and other religious women designated as laity.

3. The documents of the Second Vatican Council, as in previous Councils, are categorized according to the degree to which they are morally binding. Constitutions are considered the most binding; then decrees; and, finally, declarations. The document on renewal of religious life belongs to the second category, that of decrees. All these documents are found in Flannery 1975.

4. I have used the explanation of the Council Constitutions of Sister Helen Wright, SND de Namur, *Eschatology in the Pastoral Constitution on the Church in the Modern World*, 1972, unpublished doctoral dissertation, University of Toronto.

5. Yves Congar, one of the *periti* at the Second Vatican Council, developed the concept of "the people of God" in the early fifties in his book *Lay People in the Church*. Although it was under a ban in the 1950s, he became a major resource person in ecclesiology at the Council. When I was developing a model for examining the new directions of the church in its growing social awareness during the 1950s, the variables I selected, on the basis of their then current influence toward change in the church, were responsible use of authority; awareness of social needs and taking responsibility for addressing them; critical obedience; respect for scientific findings; and an understanding of unconscious motivation. All of these were related to a laity growing to full maturity in the church (see Neal, *Values and Interests in Social Change*, Chapter 2).

6. During the Second Vatican Council, Council watchers, like the International Documentation on the Conciliar Church (IDOC), a lay organization of religious and laity centered in Rome, published the draft documents as they were mimeographed for Council use. They translated them into at least eight different languages and mailed them to local church groups all over the world. Discussions of these documents went back and forth to Rome. The Grail, another group of dedicated laity, was a contact location for these discussions.

7. Other sisters present and actively involved at the Grail meeting in 1964 were: Jacqueline Grennan and Mary Ellen Muckenhirn, both of whom have since left religious life; Sr. Margaret Claydon and Sr. Ann Ida Gannon, both then college presidents, of Trinity College in Washington, D.C., and of Mundelein in Chicago respectively.

8. These same women became members of the national committee for the Sisters' Survey, along with five members of the national board. Thus, the committee included: Sr. Charles Borromeo (Mary Ellen) Muckenhirn, C.S.C., theologian; Sr. Elena Malits, C.S.C., theologian; Sr. M. Aloysius (Mary) Schaldenbrand, S.S.J., philosopher; Sr. Jane Marie Richardson, S.L., liturgist; Sr. Corita Kent, I.H.M., artist; Sr. Mary Angelica (Ann) Seng, O.S.F., social scientist; Sr. Jane Marie Luecke, O.S.B., poet and educator; and Sr. Marie Augusta Neal, S.N.D. de Namur, sociologist. The major superiors working with this group included: Sr. Mary Luke Tobin, S.L.; Sr. Thomas Aquinas (Elizabeth) Carroll, R.S.M.; Sr. Mary Daniel Turner, S.N.D. de Namur; Sr. Mary Isabel Concannon, C.S.J.; and Sr. Angelita Myerscough, A.D.P.P.S. Theology, philosophy, and education were their areas of training.

9. Extensive research and testing went into the construction of this measure of religious belief. It became the most controversial and the most discriminating variable, which accounted for the pace and direction of

changes in structures of the religious congregations involved in the study. Sister Elena Malits made a major contribution to the formulation of the items. See Neal 1971, for detailed analysis of the measure of religious belief.

10. For a most negative view of this entire period but one that expresses clearly the anxiety of the perspective, see Msgr. George A. Kelly's *The Battle for the American Church*, New York, Doubleday, 1979.

11. Sr. Corita Kent resigned her membership in the Immaculate Heart Congregation, continued her expressive artistic career and died of cancer in Boston in 1978. To the end, she retained her close ties with her friends in the congregation which had endured the pain of early encounters with church authorities regarding the appropriate renewal of religious life.

12. Several large congregations that remained on the periphery of the renewal in the 1970s came forth with enthusiasm for the mission of social transformation in the 1980s. Since they had not been exposed to those early conflicts, their energies were reserved for a fresh start.

13. See "Mission" and "Ministry" in *The New Dictionary of Theology*, edited by Joseph A Komonchak, Mary Collins, and Dermot A. Lane, Wilmington, Delaware: Michael Glazier, Inc., 1987.

14. The quotations cited below are taken from the following sources: School Sisters of St. Francis, *Response in Faith: Rule of Life*, 1983; Sisters of Notre Dame de Namur, *Constitutions*, 1984; Maryknoll Sisters, *Constitutions*, 1980; Medical Mission Sisters, *Constitutions*, 1980; Sisters of Loretto, *I Am the Way*, Provisional *Constitutions*, 1976; Sisters of Charity of the Blessed Virgin Mary, *Constitutions*, 1982; Sisters of the Humility of Mary, Villa Maria, Pennsylvania, *Constitutions*, 1983; Immaculate Heart of Mary of Monroe, Michigan, *Constitutions*, 1982. Immaculate Heart of Mary of Scranton, Pennsylvania, *Constitutions*, 1983.

One of the earliest groups participating in renewal designed to link new structures with their original charism was the Immaculate Heart Sisters of Los Angeles. Their goal—to celebrate life in its new directions of openness to the poor through art and music—frightened the local bishop, who was not ready for their innovative spontaneity. To ward off the opposition and possible prohibitions of church authorities, before the period of general revisions of Constitutions, they chose non-canonical status and renamed themselves the Immaculate Heart Community. Their story, from then onward, took a unique direction. Sisters Anita Caspary and Corita Kent were among their most imaginative agents of change. Their struggle helped many other groups of sisters to renew. Sociologist Helen Rose Ebaugh is currently doing a study of their experiences, in comparison to those of two other religious congregations.

15. In late 1988 the Vatican commission entitled Congregation on Religious and Secular Institutes (CRIS), changed its name to Congregation of Institutes of Consecrated Living (CICL). This is the second change of name for this organization since the Vatican Council. It was earlier called SCRIS with the first "S" standing for "Sacred."

16. See, especially, "Essential Elements in Church Teaching on Religious Life," and the decree which the Vatican Congregation for Religious and Secular Institutes (CRIS) issued on February 2, 1984. It is titled: "Religious Life and the New Code of Canon Law," published in *Origins*, Vol. 14, p. 602. The canons that apply specifically to religious life in the church include: Book II, Part III, 3, Section 1, Canons 573 through 704. Canonists provide guides to assist religious groups in interpreting the range of possibilities within the Canons: see Hite *et al.* 1985.

Chapter 4

1. In the re-test of the Sisters' Survey in 1980, the sisters were asked this question: "During the past 12 years there has been much movement in and out of religious communities. As you think back on the last twelve years would you say there is a special quality of commitment that distinguishes the religious vocation, something that you know you have even if you cannot define it?" In response, 60 percent said "yes" and another 26 percent, "probably yes." Only 3 percent said "no."

2. Adam Smith was the eighteenth-century economist who first formulated the rationale of a capitalist society. That rationale may be thought of in the following terms: Maximum material welfare for the nation will be achieved where economic activities take place in response to the stimulus of self-interest, and in the absence of social controls. (See Douglas Dowd, *Modern Economic Problems in Historical Perspective*, Boston: D.C. Heath, 1965, p. 21 and Dowd's *The Waste of Nations*, 1989).

3. Edward O.Wilson, author of *Sociobiology: A New Synthesis*, Harvard University Press, 1975, and *On Human Nature*, 1978, provides the strongest argument for the genetic control of all social behavior toward the preservation of one's own gene pool. He explicitly argues that religion is part of a self-interested cultural frame, created to preserve the advantage of some in the survival of the fittest. See especially *On Human Nature*, Chapter 8, "On Religion," and the fourth chapter in my *The Just Demands of the Poor*.

4. Those signs include: the leveling-off of world population size at about 10.5 billion after the next century; development of the technological ability to provide for this population through the development of good stewardship skills; the implications of the arms race and the need for efforts to control it; the persistence of world poverty, despite technological potential for solution; and the continuation and even increase in racism, sexism and class divisions, despite the clear affirmation of universal human rights by international, church, and civic bodies.

5. The 1980 re-test of the Sisters' Survey addressed this issue. One finding indicated that only 10 percent of sisters today accept, in their vow commitment, a form of governance that calls for submission to another person believed to be more in contact with God's will than they are themselves. Choices made indicate a sense of responsibility to participate in deliberative processes designed to reach a consensus when differences exist. This form of participative decision making is regarded as more in keeping with informed participation in carrying out gospel mandates in the mission. See items 197 and 428 in the Sisters' Survey, 1980. See also Chapter 5.

6. The Maryknoll priests are an example of a society of apostolic life. They live in community, when circumstances permit, but do not take the three vows.

7. The significance of the United Nations' Covenant on Human Rights grows as we see the developing nations claim their place in discussion of resources. That the churches had much to do with the international recognition of these rights can be seen in comparing the content of Pope John XXIII's *Pacem in Terris* with the United Nations' *International Bill of Human Rights*.

8. Paulo Freire's method, originally communicated to the West in *Pedagogy of the Oppressed* and developed in other books, including *The Politics of Education: Culture, Power and Liberation*, consists of a biblical reflection on current experiences of deprivation in poor communities. The reflection then moves toward taking action to change those conditions. He was exiled from Brazil in 1964 for using this method but was commended by the Bishops of Latin America at Medellin and by the World Council of Churches, not only for using it, but for continuing to this day to teach others to do so.

9. Andrew Greeley, Peter Berger, and Michael Novak are three committed scholars of religion who have consistently acted within the premises of capitalism's assumption of basic self-interest, and, as consistently, have challenged the usefulness of liberation theology. For the role of liberation

theology in the contemporary church in Latin America, see also Leonardo Boff, *Church: Charism and Power* (English translation by John Diercksmeier). For its extension to other countries, see Maduro and Ellis, *The Future of Liberation Theology*.

10. There are some women who think that the religious congregations will not be able to make this transition to responsible obedience. Lilliana Copp has founded a group called "Sisters For Christian Community" which offers membership in a non-canonical organization. Over 600 former sisters have joined this group. See her statement of purpose in "A Look into the Future," in *National Coalition of American Nuns* (Summer 1988), Vol. 18, No. 3.

Chapter 5

1. One such formalization of this new corporate direction is expressed as follows:

We seek to establish governmental structures which:
a. protect the rights and dignity of each person;
b. call for the participation of all members;
c. encourage the growth of a communitarian spirit;
d. enable authority to be exercised in a collaborative style;
e. can be adapted to a diversity of cultures, experiences, and needs;
f. foster communication among ourselves and with others, thus making informed participative decisions more possible.

(*Constitutions*, Sisters of Notre Dame de Namur, Art. 86, p.50, 1984.)

2. I repeat here that church law also provides for several other forms of consecrated life: those lived by hermits, virgins (the most ancient), secular institutes and societies of apostolic life. Each of these has different specifications in canon law. Furthermore, there are two kinds of religious institutes: orders and congregations. Orders are distinguished by the members' profession of solemn vows and, for women, the observance of the cloister. Women in orders are called nuns; men in the monastic orders, monks. Religious institutes, however, the type to be examined here, include some religious orders and all congregations. Congregations are distinguished by the profession of simple vows by the members, the women in these groups called "sisters." Simple vows do not require the cloister and are not as final in requiring the relinquishment of ownership of property as are solemn vows taken in orders, nor in requiring stability of community, as do Benedictines, who form a unique type (Sutera 1987). The focus of this chapter is exclusively on women in religious

congregations; that is, it is about sisters as distinct from nuns (cf. Chapter 1).

3. The problems asssociated with personal authority are analyzed and categorized later in this chapter.

4. The item from which this information was derived reads as follows: "A truly obedient religious need seek no source other than her Rule and the will of her superiors to know what she should do." Only nine percent agreed. This was item 357 in the 1980 re-test of the Sisters' Survey. See *Probe*, May/June 1981, Vol. X, No. 5, for a brief report on this survey. An update of this survey was completed in 1989.

5. Some of the studies that pursue this issue of authority in the church and in society include Lora Ann Quiñonez's *Patterns of Authority and Obedience: An Overview of Authority/Obedience Development Among U.S. Women Religious,* 1978; Cussianovich's *Religious Life and the Poor: Liberation Theology Perspectives;* 1979; Sandra Schneider's "Toward a Theology of Religious Obedience," in *Starting Points,* edited by L.A. Quiñonez, CDP, pp. 59-86; Madonna Kolbenschlag, *Kiss Sleeping Beauty Goodbye,* 1979, and *Authority, Community and Conflict,* 1986; Mary Jo Weaver's, *New Catholic Women, A Contemporary Challenge to Religious Authority,* 1985.

6. See *Probe*, March/April, Vol. X, No. 4, 1981.

7. This dialogue continues in 1988. See Lilliana Copp, NCAN, (Summer) 1988. Her proposal of non-canonical status, although an alternative for some individuals, is not the alternative sisters generally seek. The challenge for most incorporates a commitment to the structure, because religious life entails membership in a structure that moves the church in each age to the realization of its mission.

8. The Dominicans, unlike other congregations, take only one vow, that of obedience. Chastity and poverty are worked into that commitment.

9. See *Constitutions and Directory* of the Sisters of Notre Dame de Namur, 1984, Article 73, p. 39.

10. Linscott, 1983, p. 206. She is a former president of the International Union of Superiors General, and was the contact person for religious congregations of women in the area of Constitutions and General Chapters at the Congregation for Institutes of Consecrated Life in Rome.

Bibliography

Adriance, Cousineau Madeleine. *Opting for the Poor: Brazilian Catholicism in Transition*. Kansas City: Sheed and Ward, 1986.

Arruda, Marcos, ed. *Ecumenisn and a New World Order: The Failure of the 1970s and the Challenges of the 1990s*. Commission on the Churches' Participation in Development, Geneva: World Council of Churches, 1980.

Barker, Eileen. *New Religious Movements: A Perspective for Understanding Society*. New York: Edwin Mellen, 1982.

Bartunek, Jean M. "Changing Interpretive Schemes and Organizational Restructuring: The Example of a Religious Order," *Administrative Science Quarterly*, 29 (1984): 355-372.

Baum, Gregory. *Theology and Society*. Mahwah, N.J.: Paulist Press, 1987.

Berryman, Phillip. *The Religious Roots of Rebellion*. Maryknoll, N.Y.: Orbis Books, 1984.

_____. *Liberation Theology*. Philadelphia: Temple University Press, 1987.

Boff, Leonardo. *Church: Charism and Power*. New York: Crossroad, 1986.

Boyd, Catherine E.. *A Cistercian Nunnery in Medieval Italy: Story of Rifreddo in Saluzzo, 1220-1300*. Cambridge: Harvard University Press, 1943.

Bradley, Sister Rita Mary. *The Mind of the Church in the Formation of Sisters*. New York: Fordham University Press, 1960.

Brown, Lester. *State of the World*. Washington D.C.: World Watch Institute, 1986.

Bynum, Carolyn. W. *Jesus as Mother: Studies in the Spirituality of the High Middle Ages.* Berkeley: University of California Press, 1982.

Canadian Conference of Bishops. "Toward a Coalition for Development," *Strategy Committee Report, Canadian Conference of Bishops,* 1969.

Cardenal, Ernesto. *The Gospel of Solentiname.* Maryknoll, N.Y.: Orbis Books, 1976.

Catholic Bishops of the Appalachian Region. "This Land is Home to Me," *Pastoral Letter on Powerlessness in Appalachia.* Catholic Committee on Appalachia, 1974.

Charmot, F., S.J. *Society of the Sacred Heart.* Lyons: Lescuyer, 1953.

Chenu, M. D., O.P. "Toward a Theology of Work," *Cross Currents,* VII (Winter, 1957): 175-187.

Chittister, Joan, *et al. Climb Along the Cutting Edge: An Analysis of Change in Religious Life.* New York: Paulist Press, 1977.

Code of Canon Law, prepared by the Canon Law Society of Great Britain and Ireland. London: Collins, 1983. (English translation of *Codex Iuris Canonici,* promulgated by Pope John Paul II.)

Congar, Yves. *Lay People in the Church.* Westminster, Md.: Newman Press, 1957.

Cussianovich, Alejandro, S.D.B. *Religious Life and the Poor: Liberation Theology Perspectives.* Maryknoll, N.Y.: Orbis Books, 1979.

Daly, Robert J. S.J., *et al. Religious Life in the U.S.: The New Dialogue.* Mahwah, N.J.: Paulist Press, 1984.

Danielou, Jean, S.J. *The Ministry of Women in the Early Church.* Translated from *La Maison Dieu,* No. 61, Rt. Rev. Glyn Simon. New York: Morehouse-Barlow, 1960.

Davies, Stevan L. *The Revolt of the Widows.* Carbondale and Edwardsville: Southern Illinois University, 1980.

Dorr, Donal. *Option for the Poor: A Hundred Years of Vatican Social Teaching.* Maryknoll, N.Y.: Orbis Books, 1983.

Douglas, Mary. *Natural Symbols.* New York: Random House, 1972.

Douglas, Mary and Steven Tipton. *Religion and America: Spirituality in a Secular Age*. Boston: Beacon Press,1983.

Dowd, Douglas F. *Modern Economic Problems in Historical Perspective*. Boston: D. C. Heath and Company, 1965.

_____. *The Waste of Nations: The Dysfunction of the World Economy*. Boulder, Colorado: Westview Press, 1989.

Eagleson, John and Philip Scharper, eds. *Puebla and Beyond*. Maryknoll, N.Y.: Orbis Books, 1979.

Ebaugh, Helen Rose. *Out of the Cloister*. Austin: University of Texas, 1977.

Elizondo, Virgil and Norbert Greinacher, eds. *Women in a Men's Church*. New York: Seabury, 1980, *Concilium*, Vol. 134.

Evans, Alice F. and Robert A., William Bean Kennedy. *Pedagogies for the Non-Poor*. Maryknoll, New York: Orbis Books, 1987.

Ewens, Mary. *The Role of the Nun in Nineteenth-Century America*. New York: Arno, 1978.

Falk, Nancy A. and Rita M. Gross, eds. *Unspoken Worlds: Women's Religious Lives*. N.Y.: Harper & Row, 1980.

Fiorenza, Elisabeth Schüssler. "Word, Spirit and Power: Women in Early Christian Communities," in *Women of Spirit: Female Leadership in the Jewish and Christian Tradition*. Edited by Rosemary Radford Ruether. New York: Simon and Schuster, 1970.

_____. *In Memory of Her: Feminist Theological Reconstruction of Christian Origins*. New York: Crossroad, 1983.

Fitts, Mary Pauline. *Hands to the Needy: Blessed Marguerite D'Youville, Apostle to the Poor*. New York: Doubleday, 1971.

Flannery, Austin, O.P., ed. *Vatican Council II: The Conciliar and Post-Conciliar Documents*. New York: Costello, 1975.

Freire, Paulo. *Pedagogy of the Oppressed*. New York: Seabury, 1970.

_____. *The Politics of Education: Culture, Power and Liberation*. South Hadley, Massachusetts: Bergin and Garvey, 1985.

Friess, Rev. Frederick. *Life of Reverend Mother Mary Teresa of Jesus Gerhardinger: Foundress and Superior General of the Congregation of Poor School Sisters of Notre Dame.* Baltimore: St. Mary's Industrial school, 1907. (A translation from the German.)

Gallo, Jeanne, S.N.D. *Basic Ecclesial Communities: A New Form of Christian Response to the World Today.* Unpublished doctoral dissertation, Boston University, 1988.

George, Susan. *Ill Fares the Land: Essays on Food, Hunger and Power.* Washington, D.C.: Institute of Policy Studies, 1984.

Gnuse, Robert. *You Shall Not Steal.* Maryknoll, N.Y.: Orbis Books, 1986.

Grollmes, Eugene E., ed. *Vows But No Walls: An Analysis of Religious Life.* St. Louis: B. Herder, 1967.

Gutiérrez, Gustavo. *A Theology of Liberation.* Maryknoll, N.Y.: Orbis Books, 1973 (revised 1988).

Haley, Joseph E., C.S.C. *Proceedings of the 1953 Sisters' Institute of Spirituality.* Notre Dame, Ind.: University of Notre Dame Press, 1954.

Hammond, Phillip E., ed. *The Sacred in a Secular Age.* Berkeley, California: University of California Press, 1985.

Hauptman, Judith. "Images of Women in the Talmud," in *Religion and Sexism.* Edited by Rosemary Radford Ruether. New York: Simon and Schuster, 1974.

Hilpisch, Stephanus, O.S.B. *History of Benedictine Nuns.* Collegeville, Minn.: St. John's University Press, 1950.

Hite, Jordan, Sharon Holland, and Daniel Ward. *A Handbook on Canons 573-746.* Collegeville, Minn.: The Liturgical Press, 1985.

Hoge, Dean R., and Joseph J. Shields. "Changing Age Distribution and Theological Attitudes of Catholic Priests, 1970-1985," *Sociological Analysis.* Vol. 49, No. 3, Fall 1988, pp. 264–280.

John XXIII. *Mater et Magistra.* Boston: St. Paul Editions, 1961.

_____. *Peace on Earth (Pacem in Terris).* Boston: St. Paul Editions, 1963.

John Paul II. *On Human Labor* (*Laborem Exercens*). Boston: St. Paul Editions, 1981.

_____. *"Redemptionis Donum"* (*Apostolic Exhortation on Religious Life*). Boston: St. Paul Editions, 1984.

_____. *On Social Concerns* (*Sollicitudo Rei Socialis*). Boston: St. Paul Editions, 1988.

Johnson, David, M., ed. *Justice and Peace Education: Models for College and University Faculty*. Maryknoll, N.Y.: Orbis Books, 1986.

Kolbenschlag, Madonna.*Between God and Caesar: Priests, Sisters and Political Office in the United States*. Mahwah, N.J.: Paulist Press, 1985.

_____. *Authority, Community and Conflict*. Kansas City: Sheed and Ward, 1986.

Kolmer, Elizabeth. *Religious Women in the United States Since 1950: A Survey of the Literature*. Wilmington, Del.: Michael Glazier, Inc., 1984.

Lappe, Frances Moore and Joseph. *World Hunger: Ten Myths*. San Francisco: Institute for Food and Development Policy, 1985.

Latin American Bishops Second General Conference. *The Church in the Present Day Transformation of Latin America in the Light of the Council*. Position Papers, 2 Vols., Bogota, Colombia: CELAM, 1970.

Leadership Conference of Women Religious. *Widening the Dialogue: Reflection on Evangelica Testificatio*, Washington D.C., 1974.

Leo XIII. *Rerum Novarum* (*On the Conditions of Labor*). Boston: St. Paul Editions. (Originally Published, 1891.)

_____. *"Conditae a Christo,"* 1900, in *Acta Sanctae Sedis*, Vol. 33, 341-347.

Lerner, Gerta. *The Creation of Patriarchy*. New York: Oxford University Press, 1986.

Leyser, K.J. *Rule and Conflict in an Early Medieval Society*. Ottanian Saxony, Bloomington: Indiana University, 1979.

Linscott, Sister Mary. "The Service of Religious Authority: Reflections on Government in the Revision of Constitutions," *Review for Religious*, Vol. 42, No. 2 (March/April, 1983): 197-217.

de Lubac, Henri. *Catholicism: A Study of Dogma in Relationship to the Corporate Destiny of Mankind.* New York: Longmans, Green, 1950.

Maccoby, Michael. "A Psychoanalyst Looks at the Vows," in *CMSW Annual Assembly Proceedings*, 1967: 116-128.

Maduro, Otto and Marc Ellis, eds. *The Future of Liberation Theology.* Maryknoll, N.Y.: Orbis Books, 1989.

Marx, Karl and Friedrich Engels. *Basic Writings on Politics and Philosophy.* Edited by Lewis E. Feuer. New York: Doubleday, 1959.

McCarthy, Maria Caritas, S.H.C.J., Trans. *The Rule of Nuns of St. Caesarius of Arles: A Translation with Critical Introduction.* Washington, D.C.: Catholic University of America, 1960.

McLaughlin, Francis. "Morality and the Marketplace," *Boston College Magazine* (Summer, 1987): 6-7.

McNamara, Jo Ann. *A New Song: The Origins of the Female Community of Virgins in the First Three Centuries.* New York: Haworth Press, 1983.

Merton, Robert. "Unintended Consequences of Purposive Social Action," in *Social Theory and Social Structure.* New York: Free Press, 1968.

Míguez-Bonino, Jose. *Doing Theology in a Revolutionary Situation.* Philadelphia: Fortress Press, 1968.

Moore, Basil, ed. *The Challenge of Black Theology in South Africa.* Atlanta, Georgia: John Knox Press, 1974.

Muckenhirn, Mary Ellen. *The Changing Sister.* Notre Dame, Ind.: Fides Publishers, 1965.

Murphy, Elaine. *Food and Population: A Global Concern.* Washington D.C.: Population Reference Bureau, 1984.

Myers, Sr. Bertand. *Sisters from the Twenty-First Century.* New York: Sheed and Ward, 1965.

Neal, Marie Augusta, S.N.D. *Values and Interests in Social Change.* Englewood Cliffs, N. J.: Prentice Hall, 1965.

_____. "The Relation Between Religious Belief and Structural

Change in Religious Orders: Developing an Effective Measuring Instrument," *Review of Religious Research*, Part I: Vol. 12, No. 1 (Fall 1970): 2-16; Part II: Vol. 12, No. 3 (Spring 1971): 153-64.

_____. "A Theoretical Analysis of Renewal in Religious Orders in the U.S.A.," *Social Compass*, Vol. XVIII, No. 1 (1971): 7-25.

_____. "Sociological Implications for a Renewal of Religious Life," in LCWR, Ed., *Widening the Dialogue: Reflections on Evangelica Testificatio*. Washington D.C.: Leadership Conference of Women Religious, 1974.

_____. "Cultural Patterns and Behavioral Outcomes in Religious Systems: A Case Study of Religious Orders of Women in the U.S.A.," in *Religion and Social Change*.Lille, France: C.I.S.R., 1975.

_____. "Women in Religious Symbolism and Organization," in *Change and Continuity*. Edited by Harry M. Johnson. San Francisco: Jossey-Bass, 1979.

_____. "The Sisters' Survey, 1980: A Report," *Probe*, Vol. X, No. 5 (May/June), 1981.

_____. *Catholic Sisters in Transition from the 1960s to the 1980s*. Wilmington, Del.: Michael Glazier, Inc., 1984.

_____. "Commitment to Altruism in Sociological Analysis," *Sociological Analysis*. Vol. 43, No. 1 (1982), 1–22.

_____. *The Just Demands of the Poor*. Mahwah, N.J.: Paulist Press, 1987.

O'Brien, David J. and Thomas A. Shannon. *Renewing the Earth: Catholic Documents on Peace, Justice, and Liberation*. Garden City, New York: Image Books, 1977.

Paul VI. *Populorum Progressio (On the Development of Peoples)*. Boston: St. Paul Editions, 1967.

_____. *Octogesima Adveniens (A Call to Action, Apostolic Letter on the Eightieth Anniversary of Rerum Novarum)*. Washington, D.C.: United States Catholic Conference, 1971.

_____. *Evangelica Testificatio*. Boston: St. Paul Editions, 1973.

Pius XI. *Quadragesimo Anno (On the Reconstruction of the Social Order)*. Boston: St. Paul Editions, 1931.

_____. *The Christian Education of Youth.* Boston: St. Paul Editions, 1929.
Pius XII. *Sponsa Christi.* Boston: St. Paul Editions, 1950.

Ple, A. O.P.; B.R. Fulkerson, S.J.; Gerald Kelly, S.J.; Romaeus O'Brien, O. Carm. *Religious Life in the Modern World.* Notre Dame, Ind.: University of Notre Dame, 1961.

Ple, A. *Religious Life VII: The Direction of Nuns.* (The English version of *Directoire des prêtres chargés des religieuses.*) Westminster, Md.: Newman Press, 1957.

_____. *Religious Sisters.* (English edition of *Les adaptations de la vie religieuse,* prepared by A. Ple with an introduction by Cardinal Suhard.) London: Blackfriars, 1950.

Pomeroy, Sarah B. *Goddesses, Whores, Wives and Slaves: Women in Classical Antiquity.* New York: Schocken Books, 1975.

Population Reference Bureau. *1980 Population Data Sheet.* Washington, D.C.: Population Reference Bureau, 1989.

_____. *Global Population Trends: Challenges Facing World Leaders.* Washington, D.C.: Population Reference Bureau, 1986.

Power, Eileen. *Medieval English Nunneries.* Cambridge: Cambridge University Press, 1922.

_____. *Medieval Women.* London: Cambridge University Press, 1975.

Prelinger, Catherine M. "The Female Diaconate in the Anglican Church: What Kind of Ministry for Women," in Gail Malmgreen, Ed., *Religion in the Lives of English Women 1760-1930.* London and Bloomington: Indiana University Press, 1986: 161-192.

Prelinger, Catherine M., and Rosemary S. Keller. "The Function of Female Bonding: The Restored Deaconessate of the Nineteenth Century," in Rosemary S. Keller, Louise L. Queen, Hilah F. Therras, eds. *Women in New Worlds: Historical Perspectives in the Wesleyan Tradition.* Nashville, Tenn.: Abingdon Press, 1982, II: 260-315.

_____. "The Nineteenth-Century Deaconessate in Germany: The Efficacy of a Family Model," in Ruth Ellen B. Joeres and Mary Jo Maynes, eds., *Condition and Consciousness: German Women in the Eighteenth and Nineteenth Centuries.* Bloomington: Indiana University Press, 1986, 215-29.

Quiñonez, Lora Ann, C.D.P. *Starting Points: Six Basic Essays on the Experience of U.S. Women Religious.* Washington, D.C.: Leadership Conference of Women Religious, 1980.

_____. *Patterns of Authority and Obedience: An Overview of Authority/ Obedience Development Among U.S. Women Religious.* Washington, D.C.: Leadership Conference of Women Religious, 1978.

Rahner, Karl. *Inspiration in the Bible.* New York: Herder and Herder, 1961.

_____. "Reflections on Obedience," *Cross Currents,* X (Fall, 1960): 362-374.

Richard, Pablo, *et al. Idols of Death and the God of Life.* Maryknoll, N.Y.: Orbis Books, 1983.

Rothluebber, Sister Francis Borgia, O.S.F. *He Sent Two: The Story of the Beginning of the School Sisters of St. Francis.* Milwaukee, Wis.: Seraphic Press, 1965.

Ruether, Rosemary Radford. "Mothers of the Church," in *Women of Spirit: Female Leadership in the Jewish and Christian Tradition.* New York: Simon and Schuster, 1974.

_____. *New Heaven and New Earth: Sexist Ideologies and Human Liberation.* New York: Seabury, 1975.

Ruether, Rosemary Radford and Rosemary S. Keller. *Women and Religion in America in the Nineteenth Century.* New York: Harper & Row, 1981.

Russell, Letty. *Authority in Feminist Theology.* Philadelphia: Westminister Press, 1987.

Sacred Congregation of Religious. *Apostolic Constitution "Sponsa Christi" and Instruction.* Boston: St. Paul Editions, 1950.

Schneiders, Sandra M., I.H.M. "Toward a Theology of Religious Obedience," in *Starting Points.* Edited by Lora Ann Quiñonez, CDP, Washington, D.C.: Leadership Conference of Women Religious, 1980: 59-85.

Sister Jeanne Marie. *Maryknoll's First Lady.* Maryknoll, N.Y.: Orbis Books, 1964.

Sister M. Rosalita. *The Greater Service: The History of the Congregation of the Sister Servants of the Immaculate Heart of Mary.* Monroe, Michigan: 1845-1945. Detroit: (private printing) 1948.

Sister of Notre Dame. *Life of the Venerable Servant of God: Julie Billiart.* New York: Art and Book Co., 1898.

Sister of St. Joseph. *Mother Saint John Fontbonne: Foundress of the Sisters of Saint Joseph.* New York: Kennedy and Sons, 1936.

Sobrino, Jon. *Spirituality of Liberation: Toward Political Holiness.* Maryknoll, New York: Orbis Books, 1988.

Sobrino, Jon and Juan Hernandez Pico, S.S. *Theology of Christian Solidarity.* Maryknoll, N.Y.: Orbis Books, 1985.

Sutera, Judith, O.S.B. *True Daughters: Monastic Identity and American Benedictine Women's History.* Atchison, Kans.: Mount St. Scholastica, 1987.

Synod of Bishops. *Synodal Document on Justice in the World.* Second General Assembly, Rome, Nov. 30, 1971. Boston: St. Paul Editions, 1971.

Teilhard de Chardin, Pierre. *The Future of Man.* New York: Harper & Row, 1964.

Tamez, Elsa, *The Bible of the Oppressed.* Maryknoll, N.Y.: Orbis Books, 1982.

Thompson, Sally. "The Problem of Cistercian Nuns of the Twelfth and Early Thirteenth Centuries," in *Medieval Women.* Edited by Derek Baker. Oxford, England: Basil Blackwell, 1978: 227-252.

Underwood, Irene. *Catholic Sisters of the United States: Signs of Contradiction or Signs of the Times? Pro Mundi Vita: Dossiers,* No. 35, 4 (1986).

United Nations. *The International Bill of Human Rights.* New York: United Nations Information Center, 1978.

United States Catholic Conference of Bishops. "The Challenge of Peace: God's Promise and Our Response," *Origins* (May 19), 1983, Vol. 13, No. 1.

_____. "Economic Justice for All: Catholic Social Teaching and the U.S. Economy," *Origins* (Nov. 27), 1986, Vol. 16: No. 24.

_____. "Report of U.S. Bishops on Religious Life and the Decline of Vocations by the Pontifical Commission on Religious Life," *Origins* (Dec. 4), 1986, Vol. 16, No. 25: 467-470.

_____. "Partners in the Mystery of Redemption: A Pastoral Response to Women's Concerns for Church and Society," *Origins* (April 21), 1988, Vol. 17, No. 45: 758-788.

Vatican Congregation for Religious and Secular Institutes. "Essential Elements in Church Teaching on Religious Life," *Origins*, (July 7), 1983, Vol. 13, No.8: 133-142.

_____. *Ecclesiae Sanctae (Norms for Implementing the Decree on the Renewal of Religious Life)*. 1966, in Flannery, 1975, 626-633.

_____. "Religious Life and Human Promotion," *Origins* (February 5, 1981), Vol. 10, No. 34, 531-541.

Vatican Council II. *Decree on the Renewal of Religious Life (Perfectae Caritatis)*. Boston: St. Paul Editions, 1965.

_____. *Gaudium et Spes (Pastoral Constitution on the Church in the Modern World)*. In Flannery, 1975: 903-1001.

_____. *Lumen Gentium (Dogmatic Constitution on the Church)*. In *Flannery*, 1975: 350-440.

Verdieck, Mary Jeanne, Joseph J. Shields, and Dean R. Hoge. "Role Commitment Processes Revisited: American Catholic Priests, 1970-1985," *Journal for The Scientific Study of Religion* (September), 1988, Vol. 27.

Vos, Clarence J. *Women in Old Testament Worship*. Netherlands: University of Amsterdam, 1968.

Weaver, Mary Jo. *New Catholic Women: A Contemporary Challenge to Religious Authority*. New York: Harper & Row, 1985.

Weber, Max. *The Protestant Ethic and the Spirit of Capitalism*. New York: Charles Scribner, 1980 (originally, 1905).

_____. *Sociology of Religion*. Boston: Beacon Press, 1963 (originally 1922).

Wemple, Suzanne Fonay. *Women in Frankish Society, Marriage and Cloister, 500-900*. Philadelphia: University of Pennsylvania, 1981.

Wilson, Edward O. *On Human Nature*. Cambridge, Mass.: Harvard University Press, 1978.

Wilson, Janet James, ed. *Women in American Religion*. Philadelphia: University of Pennsylvania Press, 1980.

World Resources Institute. *World Resources 1987*. (An assessment of the Resource Base that supports the global economy). New York: Basic Books, 1987.

Wright, Helen, S.N.D. *Eschatology in the Pastoral of the Church in the Modern World*. Unpublished doctoral dissertation, Saint Michael's College, University of Toronto, 1972.

Zahn, Gordon. *German Catholics and Hitler's Wars*. New York: E.P. Dutton, 1969.